**DO NOT REMOVE
CARDS FROM POCKET**

The Great Bibliographers Series
edited by Norman Horrocks

1. *Ronald Brunlees McKerrow,* by John Philip Immroth. 1974.
2. *Alfred William Pollard,* by Fred W. Roper. 1976.
3. *Thomas Frognall Dibdin,* by Victor E. Neuburg. 1978.
4. *Douglas C. McMurtrie,* by Scott Bruntjen and Melissa L. Young. 1979.
5. *Michael Sadleir,* by Roy Stokes. 1980.
6. *Henry Bradshaw,* by Roy Stokes. 1984.
7. *Montague Summers,* by Frederick S. Frank. 1988.
8. *George Watson Cole,* by Donald C. Dickinson. 1990.
9. *Theodore Besterman,* by Francesco Cordasco. 1992
10. *David Anton Randall,* by Dean H. Keller. 1992.

DAVID ANTON RANDALL
1905–1975

by

Dean H. Keller

The Great Bibliographers Series, No. 10

The Scarecrow Press, Inc.
Metuchen, N.J., & London
1992

Frontispiece: David A. Randall

British Library Cataloguing-in-Publication data available

Library of Congress Cataloging-in-Publication Data

Randall, David Anton, 1905-1975.
  David Anton Randall, 1905-1975 / [edited, with an essay] by
Dean H. Keller.
    p.   cm. -- (The Great bibliographers series ; no. 10)
  Includes bibliographical references and index.
  ISBN 0-8108-2624-0 (acid-free paper)
  1. Antiquarian booksellers--United States. 2. Rare books--
United States. 3. Rare book libraries--United States. 4. Lilly
Library (Indiana University, Bloomington). 5. Rare book libraries
--Indiana--Bloomington. 6. Randall, David Anton, 1905-1975. I.
Keller, Dean H. II. Title. III. Series.
Z479.R34 1992
381'.45002'0973--dc20   92-37011

DEDICATED TO

The Family of

David Anton Randall

***

The Staff, Past and Present, of

The Lilly Library

***

My Colleagues at the

Kent State University Libraries

CONTENTS

ACKNOWLEDGMENTS

Grateful acknowledgment is made to:

AB Bookman's Weekly for permission to reprint "Book Collecting as a Hobby" April 11, 1953; "IPEX" September 30, 1963; and "J.K. Lilly--America's Quiet Collector" June 27, 1966.

The Book Collector for permission to reprint "Josiah Kirby Lilly" Autumn, 1957; review of *Victorian Detective Fiction* Summer, 1967; and "Query 267. Ian Fleming's First Book" Autumn, 1972.

College & Research Libraries, the American Library Association, for permission to reprint the review of *Suppressed Commentaries on the Wiseian Forgeries* July, 1970.

The Lilly Library for permission to reprint the following: the *Tamerlane* section from *The J.K. Lilly Collection of Edgar Allan Poe*, 1964; the "Preface" to *Grolier: or 'Tis Sixty Years Since*, 1963; and "Notes on Rarity" from *Three Centuries of American Poetry*, 1965.

The *Papers of the Bibliographical Society of America* for permission to reprint the following: "Doyle, A. Conan (1879-1928). Memoirs of Sherlock Holmes" 2nd Quarter, 1940; "Thackeray, W.M. (1811-1836). Vanity Fair" 2nd Quarter, 1940; "Bruce Rogers' First Decorated Book" 1st Quarter, 1961; "A Plea for a More Consistent Policy of Cataloguing by Auction Galleries" 2nd Quarter, 1946; and review of *Bibliographical Resources for the Study of Nineteenth Century English Fiction*, 2nd Quarter, 1965.

Publisher's Weekly, published by the R.R. Bowker Company, for permission to reprint the following: review of *An Inquiry into the Nature of Certain Nineteenth Century Pamphlets* July 7, 1934, copyright 1934 by R.R. Bowker Company; "Kipling and Collecting" January 25, 1936, copyright 1936 by R.R. Bowker Company; review of *Merle Johnson's American First Editions*, November 28, 1936, copyright 1936 by R.R. Bowker Company; and "The Hogan Sale of American Literature" November 25, 1944, copyright 1944 by R.R. Bowker Company.

The Department of Special Collections, University Research Library, University of California at Los Angeles for permission to reprint "The Sadleir Collection" from *The Sadleir Collection: Addresses Delivered by Frederick B. Adams, Jr. and David A. Randall at the Dedication Ceremonies, University of California at Los Angeles Library, November 13, 1952,* 1953.

Ronald R. Randall for generously making available writings of his father, David A. Randall.

PREFACE

Dave Randall might very well have been the first to question his place in a series of books on "The Great Bibliographers." He was a practical bookman, both as a dealer in rare books and as a rare book librarian. His writings centered, for the most part, on the practical, historical, and anecdotal side of books, and his intelligence, knowledge, and enthusiasm informed everything he said and wrote. The essays, reviews, and notes reprinted in this volume, the checklist of his writings, and the account of the people and events he was associated with amply attest to the significance of his work and ideas and they place him securely in the annals of bibliography and librarianship.

Many persons contributed to making this book possible. In addition to those publishers who are acknowledged elsewhere for granting permission to reprint some of Dave Randall's writings, I owe a great debt of gratitude to Ronald R. Randall for making available his outstanding collection of his father's books, articles, correspondence, and memorabilia, and for his graceful foreword to this book. Without his very active support, and the contributions by his brother Bruce E. Randall and his cousin David V. Randall, this book would have been less accurate and complete.

The Lilly Library at Indiana University in Bloomington is a great resource for information about Dave Randall and about The Lilly Library during his tenure there. Special thanks to Lilly Librarian William R. Cagle for his interest in this project, for granting access to the archives held in his library, and for reading portions of this work in manuscript. I am also grateful to Joel Silver and other members of the staff of The Lilly Library for their assistance. I also wish to thank Jacob Chernofsky, editor of *AB Bookman's Weekly*, and Alex Gildzen, Curator of Special Collections and Archives at the Kent State University Libraries for their interest and assistance.

Dean H. Keller
Kent State University Libraries
Kent, Ohio

FOREWORD

To write a note, for publication, about one's father involves travelling both subjective and objective paths. The hope is that, trending from the same source, they will if not meet, at least rather neatly parallel.

As early as I can remember books have been a part of my life. I was fortunate to have been an early reader and this blessing was nurtured by my father: books for birthdays, books for Christmas and books without any reason at all. The time was just before World War II and the distractions of the day were few. There was film, but in a small town the picture changed only once a week. There was radio, of course, but not today's media blast of instant communications and that great visual distraction: television. It was a slower time, in retrospect a gentler time. Reading was what one did: it entertained, it educated and it met with approval from parent and teacher.

My father would sometimes bring home a treasure to show us or work on a catalogue at home on a weekend or briefly bring to the house a small library acquired in the vicinity. It was a treat to make the twenty-mile trip into Manhattan and visit the premises of the famous firm of Charles Scribner's on Fifth Avenue. Dad's underlit sanctum located down a few steps at the rear of the main floor was a special place of wonder. It contained, as I now fully realize, one of the great stocks of rare books in the world. Thus I had some exposure to the commercial aspect of books, though it never made as much impression on me as I could wish for now!

Perhaps my fondest memory is of long summer evenings when chapters from some engrossing book were read aloud with the family gathered in the living room or on the screen porch which ran the length of the front of our house. My mother especially was a wonderful reader. Indeed, both parents contributed to a literary bent in their offspring. I've now spent a delightful quarter century in the rare book business while my brother Bruce, in addition to varied other accomplishments (Mr. Universe, professional football coach, noted Tiffany glass collector) is a published author.

As a teenager the inevitable competitions for my time increased, but I never really ceased reading. To this day, I won't get into a long bank line, visit a doctor's office or--most important--step aboard a train or airplane without something to read. It may be called an addiction, it is certainly a source of great companionship. However one terms it, I'm grateful to my father for opening the door to the fascinating world of books: it is the gift for a lifetime.

Ronald R. Randall

PART I

DAVID ANTON RANDALL, 1905-1975

In a span of forty-six years, David A. Randall successfully engaged in two careers. From 1929 until 1955 he was a dealer of rare books in New York City, and from 1956 until his death in 1975 he was the head of the rare book library, The Lilly Library, at Indiana University. While the two careers are obviously related, moving from one to the other is not always easy, but David Randall had a talent and temperament to be able to make significant contributions in both areas.

Dave Randall was born on April 5, 1905, in Nanticoke, Pennsylvania, a borough in Luzerne County about seven miles down the Susquehanna River from Wilkes-Barre in the heart of the rich anthracite region. He was the son of David Virgil and Harriet Witt Randall. His father was a coal company executive, a career followed by Randall's older brother, Harradon. At the time of his death in 1930, David Virgil Randall was general manager of the thirteen anthracite collieries owned by the M. A. Hanna Company of Cleveland. At home young David was known as Anton and after he entered the Harrisburg Academy it was always Dave, and that is how he was addressed throughout the rest of his life.

Young Randall attended Harrisburg Academy, where Morton Thompson, the future author of *The Cry and the Covenant* and *Not as a Stranger*, was classmate and close friend, and he was graduated cum laude from the school in 1924. He then entered Lehigh University in nearby Bethlehem, Pennsylvania, as did his brother before him, where he received his B. A. in English in 1928 with an undergraduate thesis on Malory's *Morte d'Arthur*. At Lehigh he was a member of the Phi Delta Theta fraternity and the Phi Beta Kappa honor society. It was also at Lehigh that his interest in books, and especially rare books, was stimulated, for he worked in the University's library as an assistant to Dr. Robert

3

Metcalf Smith, a professor of English, who was conducting research on the Shakespeare folios which were in Lehigh's library collection. Smith's research was published by Lehigh in 1927 as *The Shakespeare Folios and the Forgeries of Shakespeare's Handwriting in the Lucy Packer Linderman Memorial Library of Lehigh with a list of Folios in American Libraries*. Involved in Smith's research as he was, Randall was exposed to the names, at least, of the great collectors, scholars, book dealers, and libraries which Smith contacted, cited and discussed in his monograph. Years later, in 1945, Randall was instrumental in helping his former professor have his somewhat controversial book, *The Shelley Legend*, published by Scribner's, a favor which Smith duly acknowledged in his "Preface." Formal recognition of Smith's influence was made when Randall named him one of the dedicatees of his memoirs, *Dukedom Large Enough*.

Randall retained his ties to Lehigh University and in 1966 he was appointed to the Visiting Committee of the Lehigh University Library. In that same year, on October 9, the University conferred an Honorary Doctor of Letters degree upon him.

Immediately upon graduation from Lehigh in 1928, Randall turned down a Rhodes Scholarship and entered Harvard Law School. He soon found that he couldn't give his full attention to the law and that he was drawn more and more to the world of books. He spent his time at Harvard in the Widener Library and as an auditor in a course called "History of the Printed Book" taught by George Parker Winship. Winship, a distinguished Harvard librarian, bibliographer, and author, taught this popular course between 1915 and 1931, and is credited with stimulating the book collecting instincts of many Harvard undergraduates. By January 1929, Randall had withdrawn from Harvard and was employed by E. Byrne Hackett at the Brick Row Book Shop in New York. Winship had given him a letter of introduction to Edgar H. Wells, but Wells had no openings and referred Randall to Hackett. His immediate boss at Brick Row was Michael Papantonio, later the partner of John S. Van E. Kohn in the distinguished Seven Gables Bookshop, and his first assignment was to attend the Jerome Kern sale which went through ten sessions beginning on January 7, 1929. Before the sale Randall had been given the opportunity to use a small room off Kern's library in order to examine some of the more important sale items. Kern's *Showboat* was a hit on

Broadway at the time and the composer was then at work on his next show, *Sweet Adeline*, which would star Helen Morgan, the Julie in *Showboat*. Randall kept the door to his small room open so he could hear members of the cast of *Showboat* refurbish their performances under Kern's demanding tutelage. He also heard Helen Morgan try out songs from *Sweet Adeline*, including "Why Was I Born?" which remained one of Randall's favorites. Thus Randall was thrust into the rare book business at the highest level and soon he was introduced to the great collectors, dealers, and rare book librarians of that exciting era.

While the era was an exciting one for the rare book business, it also was the beginning of the Great Depression and soon less attention, and financial resources, could be given to book collecting. Book shops were retrenching and in 1931, on Christmas Eve, Hackett told Randall his services would no longer be needed. Randall had made a good beginning in the trade at Brick Row, Mike Papantonio was a fine mentor, and he had cultivated a wide acquaintance in the trade, but the fact was that no one in the book business was hiring.

An alternative to returning to the coal fields of Eastern Pennsylvania, and the one which Randall chose, was to become a book scout. Working out of his home on East 10th Street just off Fourth Avenue in New York, he combed the secondhand bookshops which then lined Fourth Avenue between 8th and 14th streets for books needed by the "tonier" dealers in the trade. It was the scout's business to know the interests and specialities of the dealers, what books they had and what they needed, and, most importantly when one's livelihood depended upon it, what they were willing to pay. With the knowledge he had gained while at Brick Row, his considerable innate ability, and a good deal of luck, Randall was a successful scout, but he realized his future as such would be limited and the work was definitely not certain enough on which to raise a family. On July 12, 1929, Randall and Margaret Rauch had been married and their first son, Bruce Emerson, was born on August 17, 1931. A second son, Ronald Rauch, was born January 24, 1933.

The Randalls' marriage ended in divorce after 26 years and on November 23, 1956, he married Mary Altmiller, "Polly," his sweetheart from their high school days. He was her third husband. Randall's eldest son, Bruce, won the Mr. Universe title in 1959 and subsequently traveled around the country as a member of Montgomery Ward & Co.'s sports advisory staff speaking to over a quarter of a million high school students about physical fitness. He is the author of *The Barbell Way to Physical Fitness*, developed fitness programs for professional football teams including the Washington Redskins, and he is an internationally known collector of Tiffany glass. Younger son Ronald followed in his father's footsteps as a dealer in rare books. He served his apprenticeship with Warren R. Howell in San Francisco's famous John Howell--Books, and then, in 1977, joined John Windle to form Randall & Windle. The firm changed its name to Randall House in 1979 and in 1987 it moved to Santa Barbara, California.

Near the end of his first year as a book scout, Randall was discussing his ambitions with Max Harzof, the owner of G. A. Baker & Company, Booksellers, at 480 Lexington Avenue in New York, when Harzof, with the generosity that evidently marked his dealing with other aspiring bookmen, offered Randall a desk in his shop and access to his books. In return, Randall helped with cataloguing, ran errands, and performed other chores as they came up. Years later Randall called Harzof "the finest all-around bookman I have been privileged to know"[1] and he said that "I worked harder, earned less and learned more in the three years I spent with him than [in] any other comparable period."[2]

From his desk at G. A. Baker & Company, Randall issued his first two catalogues, printed by Peter Beilenson, and filled mostly with books from Harzof's stock, and it was there that he met Frederick B. Adams, Jr., John Carter, H. Bacon Collamore, William A. Jackson, J. K. Lilly, Jr., William Mitchell Van Winkle, and John T. Winterich, all of whom would have considerable influence on his career. It was during this period, too, that he began to write book reviews and articles on bibliography and book collecting, including "American First Editions, 1900-1933," in a groundbreaking collection of essays edited by John Carter called *New Paths in Book Collecting*.

John Carter was employed by Scribner's as their London buyer of rare books, and he had been urging the firm to reorganize the rare book department at the New York shop along the lines he advocated in his book. He believed a new clientele of younger collectors with a little money and a lot of imagination could be attracted. Charles Scribner agreed with the idea and a search was begun for a manager of the reorganized department. The great collector of Horace Walpole, Wilmarth Lewis, whom Randall had met at Harzof's, recommended Randall for the job, seconded, it seems, by John Carter. Charles Scribner was quick to decide and in 1935 Dave Randall began his twenty-year tenure as manager of the Rare Book Department of Charles Scribner's Sons' New York bookstore. This also marked the beginning of what Randall later dubbed the "Carter-Randall Scribner axis"[3] that resulted in the location and sale of so many great, rare, and unusual books and manuscripts in the next two decades. From the beginning Randall and Carter determined to offer books that illustrated the philosophy demonstrated in *New Paths of Book Collecting*. While they did not neglect the more traditional areas of collecting, a review of the catalogues they issued reveal a determination vigorously to pursue new paths as well.

Randall's first catalogue, number 102 in the Scribner series issued in 1935, was *Familiar Quotations: A Collection of Their Earliest Appearances*, perhaps inspired by one of Carroll A. Wilson's favorite collecting areas, and the last major catalogue was *Fifty Distinguished Books and Manuscripts*, number 137 issued in 1952, the only dealer's catalogue in our century, Randall believed, to list a Gutenberg Bible.[4] In between there were many exciting, unusual, and groundbreaking catalogues, including one devoted to first editions of books published by Charles Scribner's Sons from 1847 to 1936 (number 108), and a 1936 catalogue called *First Editions of Juvenile Fiction, 1814-1924* (number 107) with a Harry Castlemon item which started J. K. Lilly, Jr. on his great Castlemon collection which later became the basis of Jacob Blanck's bibliography of Castlemon. There was *The Modern Library in First Editions*, 1938 (number 117) in that series' famous format,[5] followed by a less successful *The Limited Editions Club in First Editions*, 1939 (number 123), a superb *Catalogue of Original Manuscripts, and First Editions and Other Important Editions of the Tales of Sherlock Holmes...*, 1937 (unnumbered), two catalogues devoted to science and medicine (numbers 113 and 124), and seven catalogues of music material (numbers 105, 112, 119, 120, 121, 127 and 133).

While Randall began to publish articles and book reviews from his desk at Harzof's, the more stable and certain situation at

Scribner's encouraged him to become even more involved in writing. From 1935 to 1939 he was the American editor of *Bibliographical Notes and Queries* which was published in London by the firm of Elkin Mathews and he contributed a substantial number of notes to it. He and several others jointly conducted the "Bibliographical Notes" department of the *Papers of the Bibliographical Society of America* beginning with the second quarter of 1940 through 1941. He edited "Bibliographical Notes" for six issues of *The Baker Street Journal* in 1946-1948, and he was a contributing editor of the *New Colophon* during 1948-1950. He continued to review books for *Publishers' Weekly* and he collaborated with John T. Winterich on a series called "One Hundred Good Novels" which ran in that journal from May 1939 to March 1942. He also assisted Winterich in revising his *A Primer of Book-Collecting* in 1946 and again in 1966 and it remains one of the most readable and stimulating handbooks of its kind.

In the *Papers of the Bibliographical Society of America* for the second quarter of 1946, Randall contributed a provocative article called "A Plea for a More Consistent Policy of Cataloguing by Auction Galleries." Although Randall later said the article "had about as much effect as a feather dropped in the Grand Canyon would have towards filling it up,"[6] he received appreciative letters from H. Bacon Collamore, Arthur Houghton, Jr., Parkman D. Howe, Percy H. Muir, Howard Peckham, Carl H. Pforzheimer, Donald G. Wing, and John Cook Wyllie regarding it.

Another example of Randall's knowledge of books is his winning of *Vanity Fair* magazine's literary quiz called "The Permanent Questionnaire." The questions appeared in volume 44, August, 1935, pages 36 and 37 and the answers, with Randall's picture, appeared in the issue for October, 1935, on pages 54, 61, and 62. The notification that he had won the contest came in a telegram on September 19, 1935, and it read:

PLEASE ACCEPT FORMAL FELICITATIONS ON WINNING FIRST PRIZE IN OUR PERMANENT QUESTIONNAIRE STOP VERY SLIGHT REWARD FOLLOWS WITH ADMIRING WISHES FROM THE EDITORS OF VANITY FAIR.

Jacob Blanck and Edward Lazare shared the "very slight reward" with Randall, a token to their help on the project.

As early as 1932, in Philip Brooks' column in the *New York Times Book Review* for December 11, Randall's discoveries regarding the American edition of *Alice's Adventures in Wonderland* were noted, and Avery Strakosch, a free-lance writer who ghosted some of Dr. A. S. W. Rosenbach's articles, profiled Randall in *Avocations, A Magazine of Hobbies and Leisure,* April, 1938. Later he was featured in a *Saturday Evening Post* article, March 22, 1952, by Pete Martin who was also an avid collector of the works of George Alfred Henty.

During the Scribner years Randall's bibliographical abilities were engaged to produce a major bibliography and a collection catalogue in collaboration with collectors with whom he had worked for many years. In 1936 he was listed on the title-page of William Mitchell Van Winkle's *Henry William Herbert (Frank Forester): A Bibliography of His Writings* for providing "bibliographical assistance." Van Winkle, a prominent New York lawyer and important collector of sporting books, had met Randall at Harzof's and their friendship and business relationship continued at Scribner's. Van Winkle's law firm later came to represent Scribner author Thomas Wolfe.

Randall knew Carroll Atwood Wilson during nearly all of his collecting career, roughly from 1925 until his death in 1947. After the collector's death, his widow Jean and Randall assembled and edited Wilson's notes and descriptions of his books and Scribner's published them privately in 1950 in two volumes as *Thirteen Author Collections of the Nineteenth Century and Five Centuries of Familiar Quotations.* Randall kept an interleaved copy of the catalogue in which he recorded the names of purchasers of many of the books and the prices paid for them.

Randall's knowledge of books enabled him to be helpful and useful to a number of authors and compilers of bibliographies and exhibition catalogues, and he was often generously praised and thanked for his work. His friend Jacob Blanck acknowledged Randall's assistance in his "Preface" to *Peter Parley to Penrod: A Bibliographical Description of the Best-Loved American Juvenile Books,* New York, R. R. Bowker, 1938, and inscribed a copy for him. Carroll A. Wilson thanked him for his assistance in an exhibition catalogue called *First Appearance in Print of Some Four Hundred Familiar Quotations,* Middletown, Connecticut, Wesleyan University, 1935, and *You Know These Lines: A Bibliography of*

the Most Quoted Verses in American Poetry, New York, G. A.
Baker & Company, 1935, is inscribed for Randall by its author,
Merle Johnson. In 1947 New York's Grolier Club issued an
exhibition catalogue called *One Hundred Influential American
Books Printed Before 1900* and Frederick B. Adams, Jr., Thomas
W. Streeter, and Carroll A. Wilson inscribed a copy "For David A.
Randall / in appreciation of his generous / contribution to this
exhibition."

This catalogue of *One Hundred Influential American Books
Printed Before 1900* was just one of the many lists of books which
collectors liked to use to build their libraries. It was one of the
methods of collecting which was argued against by John Carter
and his colleagues in *New Paths in Book Collecting*, but dealers
still had customers who liked to use the lists. Barton Currie has a
chapter in his *Fishers of Books*, Boston, Little, Brown & Company,
1931, called "Collecting by Lists." Randall's copy is heavily
annotated and the pages containing the Grolier Club, A. Edward
Newton, William Lyon Phelps, and Currie's own lists are provided
with marginal tabs for quick reference.

During his career as a book dealer, Dave Randall handled
literally thousands of books. He learned the quality of the content
of many of them, and he understood their bibliographical make-up
and printing and publishing history. He also developed strong
opinions about book collecting and book collectors, about libraries
and librarians, and about the book trade. He also had the uncanny
ability to get the right book to the right person at the right time, an
ability, it should be said, that characterizes the best librarians as
well as the best book dealers.

Much of Randall's knowledge and many of his opinions are
distilled in his 1969 volume of reminiscences called *Dukedom
Large Enough* which covers the period from 1929 to 1956, but this
knowledge and his opinions were developed, tested, and displayed in a steady stream of publications which he contributed to the
popular and scholarly press not only during his career as a book
dealer but also as the head of the Lilly Library at Indiana University.

From the Rare Book Department at Scribner's there flowed
countless books and manuscripts, singly or as collections, to
America's greatest collectors and libraries. Collectors C. Waller
Barrett, Mrs. Edward Doheny, Frank J. Hogan, Arthur A. Houghton,
Jr., J. K. Lilly, Jr., H. Bradley Martin, Morris L. Parrish, Robert H.

Taylor, and Carroll A. Wilson, libraries such as the Houghton, Huntington, Morgan, New York Public, University of California at Los Angeles, University of Virginia, and many others acquired major books and manuscripts through Randall at Scribner's. He handled such individual treasures as the Shuckburgh copy of the Gutenberg Bible, the Declaration of Independence, a copy of the Thirteenth Amendment to the Constitution signed by President Lincoln and thirty-three senators and one hundred and fourteen representatives, Poe's *The Murders in the Rue Morgue*, the manuscript of the earliest known version of Burns' "Auld Lang Syne," the manuscript of Mozart's "Haffner" symphony, Blake's *Jerusalem*, and Michael Sadleir's incomparable collection of nineteenth-century fiction, Major J. R. Abbey's collection of illustrated books, A. E. Housman's manuscripts, and Carroll A. Wilson's collection of nineteenth-century American literature.

In *Dukedom Large Enough*, on pages 28 and 29, Randall says he took the job at Scribner's at $70 a week and that at the time he was among the best paid employees in the rare book business. He also says he never made a five-figure salary in all his years at Scribner's, but he did receive an income as a stockholder and officer in various coal companies organized by his brother, Harradon. Times were undoubtedly hard in the beginning, but this income enabled Randall to concentrate more fully on the book business and worry less about day-to-day expenses than might otherwise have been the case.

Dave Randall first met J. K. Lilly, Jr. in 1932 when Max Harzof sent him to Indianapolis with a case of books to offer to the collector. Most of the books that were offered were historical Americana, not one of Lilly's greatest interests at that time, but there were also some good literary items in the case and these Randall was able to leave in Indiana. It wasn't until Randall had moved to Scribner's that his relationship with Mr. Lilly really flourished. Lilly concentrated on English and American literature, he bought one book at a time, and usually inspected everything personally before making a purchase. Lilly bought very little during the war, but in 1946 he began to collect again with an interest in medicine, science, and Americana.

Complementing Mr. Lilly's book collecting passion was his interest in bibliography and over the years he involved himself as a sponsor of several projects, to most of which Dave Randall was

connected in one way or another. We have already noted Jacob
Blanck's work on the Harry Castlemon bibliography, and Lilly was
to ask Blanck to come to Indianapolis to help with the bibliography
of James Whitcomb Riley which he was sponsoring through the
Indiana Historical Society. Lilly also supported the *Catalogue of
the Library of Thomas Jefferson*, but perhaps his greatest effort
was in the establishment and funding of the *Bibliography of
American Literature*, spearheaded again by Jacob Blanck and with
Dave Randall on the committee appointed to administer Lilly's
grant.

Plans for the *Bibliography of American Literature* project
began to take shape in 1943 based upon a plan drawn up by
Carroll A. Wilson and presented to the Council of the
Bibliographical Society of America. The project was completed
with the publication of volume nine in 1991. J. K. Lilly, Jr. had let it
be known that the Lilly Foundation would consider funding such a
project and evidently a committee consisting of Carroll A. Wilson,
chair, with Frederick B. Adams, Jr., Clarence S. Brigham, William
A. Jackson, David A. Randall, Thomas W. Streeter, and Robert W.
G. Vail was suggested to oversee the use of the grant. When the
committee was officially announced, Mr. Lilly, in a letter to Jacob
Blanck dated November 5, 1943, was "...puzzled by the fact that
our effete eastern friends saw fit to omit the name of David Randall
from the suggested committee to handle the bibliographical grant.
Also I noticed that the name of Frederick Adams, Jr. is
conspicuous by its absence for the so-called temporary
committee." Blanck responded the next day in a letter to Lilly that
"The reason for the absence of Dave Randall's name from the list is
simply this: he isn't a member of the BSA Council and, usually,
BSA committee members are Council members. This also
accounts for the omission of Fred. Adams, Jr. In Dave's case,
however, the situation is 'aggravted' [sic] by the fact that the BSA-
Grolier Club combination has a strange and archaic feeling about
booksellers that I can't even attempt to explain on rational
grounds." Lilly sent Blanck's letter of November 6 on to Randall
with his own letter, dated November 8, saying that he is "really very
much disturbed by this denouement and something more than
annoyed." In a very short time Randall received a letter from
Thomas W. Streeter, President of the Bibliographical Society of
America, dated December 1, 1943, asking him to serve on the

committee for the bibliography. Randall accepted on December 3 and joined Carroll A. Wilson, James T. Babb, Clarence S. Brigham, and William A. Jackson in overseeing the most ambitious American bibliographical project since Charles Evans began the *American Bibliography* at the beginning of this century.[7]

In 1954 Lilly confided in Randall that he was considering giving up book collecting and donating his books and manuscripts to Indiana University. Would Randall consider giving up the trade to become the curator? Randall described the factors that went into his decision in *Dukedom Large Enough*:

> I had been in the business for over a quarter-century and thought that was enough. I had had some years of commuting (from New York to Cos Cob, Connecticut, then an hour and a half each way from door to door), apartment living, Long Island living, club living, a private home in the heart of New York--all of which made a beautiful university campus seem infinitely attractive. Besides, I had gone into my profession in the first place because I liked to be around books which, individually, I could never have aspired to. But the trouble was (or so I rationalized), someone was always buying them and taking them away just as we were becoming friends. Here I could get them and keep them-- and what a lot of old friends I had to begin with. I never regretted my decision.[8]

And so it happened that on July 1, 1956, Dave Randall became Rare Book Librarian and Professor of Bibliography at Indiana University in Bloomington, thus beginning his second career in the world of books.

Indiana University already had a significant rare book collection which was located in rooms in the main library building, but in 1975, the year in which Randall died, the collection had more than doubled and was housed in its own building, The Lilly Library. The Lilly Library opened its doors to the public on Saturday, June 4, 1960, and its formal dedication took place on October 3, 1960, with President Herman B Wells presiding and with an address by Frederick B. Adams, Jr., Director of the Pierpont Morgan Library. For the dedication Randall assembled approximately 500 books and manuscripts representative of the Library's major fields of collecting at that time.

In the five years between his arrival on the Bloomington

campus and the opening of The Lilly Library, Randall set his stamp on the future direction of the Library's collections. Not only did Lilly's great collection come to Indiana University at this time, but Randall also acquired the fine collection of early printed books of George A. Poole, Jr., of Chicago, which included the New Testament portion of the Gutenberg Bible and the first Caxton printing of Chaucer's *Canterbury Tales*, the archives of the Howard Shipyards and Dock Company of Jeffersonville, Indiana, of over a quarter of a million pieces spanning the period from 1841 to 1941, and the papers of Upton Sinclair numbering nearly 200,000 items, among other large and important collections. He also acquired such important individual books and manuscripts as the first Bible in English to be printed in America, the rare first issue of *Alice's Adventures in Wonderland* by Lewis Carroll, a manuscript translation, in French, of the memoirs of James II, one of Randall's earliest accessions, the manuscript of Harold Pinter's *The Caretaker*, and Mrs. Ann S. Stephens' *Malaeska: The Indian Wife of the White Hunter*, the first in Beadle's Dime Novels series.

After the opening of The Lilly Library and during the final fifteen years of his tenure at Indiana University, Randall maintained this almost incredible record of quality and quantity of acquisitions. Among the many major collections acquired were the Bernardo Mendel library of material on Latin American discovery, history, and culture, the Starr collection of over 100,000 pieces of American popular music, the stock of the New York bookseller Lathrop C. Harper, Inc., which increased The Lilly Library's holdings of incunabula by over 400 titles, Ian Fleming's library of 19th century science and thought together with the manuscripts and his personal copies of the James Bond 007 stories, the Bobbs-Merrill publishing company archives containing over 50,000 letters, the papers of Wendell Willkie, and C. R. Boxer's collection of books and manuscripts relating to the history of the Portuguese in the East during the 17th and 18th centuries, historical works on Japan from 1542 to 1800, and the Dutch East India Company and the 17th century Anglo-Dutch naval wars. The Lilly Library always welcomed collections relating to Indiana writers, great favorites of Mr. Lilly, political figures, and distinguished Indiana University professors. Individual items acquired during these years included Tycho Brahe's *Astronomiae Instauratae Mechanica*, all four editions, each substantially revised, of Burton's *The Anatomy of*

Melancholy published during his lifetime, the manuscript of *The Adventures of the Red Circle*, a Sherlock Holmes story by Sir Arthur Conan Doyle, a personal favorite of Randall who was a member of the Baker Street Irregulars and a devoted Holmesian,[9] a diary of Theodore Dreiser covering the period of October, 1902 - February, 1903, the personal gift of Randall who made several important donations to The Lilly Library over the years, an inscribed copy of the first edition of Anna Sewell's *Black Beauty*, the manuscript of John Millington Synge's *The Playboy of the Western World*, an autograph letter of George Washington, dated April 14, 1789, in which he accepts the Presidency of the United States, and the first edition of William Butler Yeats' first book, *Mosada*. Randall was also very proud of what turned out to be his last major purchase, the first edition of John Bunyan's *The Pilgrim's Progress*.

To carry out the work of The Lilly Library, Randall was fortunate in the support he received from President and later Chancellor Herman B Wells, librarians Robert A. Miller, Cecil K. Byrd, and W. Carl Jackson, and rare book staff already in place, such as Doris Reed, Elfrieda Lang, and Geneva Warner, Josiah Q. Bennett whom Randall brought to The Lilly Library from the Parke-Bernet Galleries in New York in 1965, and William R. Cagle, now Head of The Lilly Library, who came from Indiana's main library. Together they acquired, catalogued, and made available to the scholarly community a vast array of books and manuscripts and in the process The Lilly Library quickly became known as one of the country's premier rare book libraries.

Further evidence of Randall's acquisitions work can be found in the series of *Reports* he issued from 1957 through 1969 and in the series of exhibition catalogues he produced for The Lilly Library. These *Reports* and the catalogues to which he contributed are listed in the bibliography in Part III of this book, but some of the catalogues should be singled out for special comment.

The opening of The Lilly Library focused a considerable amount of national attention on Indiana's strong holdings in many fields of study, and many groups and organizations made arrangements to visit. When possible, special exhibitions were arranged to suit the interests of the visitors. For example, in 1963 the Grolier Club visited Bloomington and the members were treated to an exhibition and catalogue entitled *Grolier: or 'Tis Sixty Years Since. A Reconstruction of the Exhibit of 100 Books Famous in English Literature Originally Held in New York, 1903*, and the following year the Manuscripts Society held its annual meeting at Indiana University and viewed an exhibition called *Manuscripts Ancient-Modern* and received a printed catalogue as a keepsake of the event. Catalogues of exhibitions of *Three Centuries of American Poetry* (1965), *Medicine* (1966), *The First Twenty-five Years of Printing* (1967), *American Patriotic Songs* (1968), *The Ian Fleming Collection* (1970), *The First Hundred Years of Detective Fiction, 1841-1941* (1973), and *Science Fiction and Fantasy* (1975), Randall's last, are important contributions and are worthy of study today.

In 1973 Randall mounted an exhibition called *Printing and the Mind of Man* based upon an exhibition with the same title which had been held in London ten years earlier. The Lilly Library lent thirty-one books to the London exhibition, over half the total sent from America, and was the fourth in the number of items contributed overall. In the catalogue of the London exhibition, Randall is listed as a member of the "Committee of Honour," and in the expanded version of that catalogue Randall and William R. Cagle are acknowledged as two who "contributed many of the American entries."[10] Randall's copy of the 1967 catalogue is inscribed by compilers John Carter and Percy H. Muir to "our adjutant general for the United States." The noted English collector and novelist Ian Fleming was third with forty-four contributions, and since Fleming's collection later came to The Lilly Library, that brought the total of actual copies exhibited owned by Lilly to seventy-five. Since The Lilly Library had not exhibited material from across the broad range of its collections since the dedication in 1960, this seemed like a good opportunity for such a review. The speaker at the opening of the 1973 exhibition at Bloomington was Nicholas Barker of Oxford University who characterized the Lilly collection and exhibition as the summit of Randall's notable career and called it an achievement that few could ever hope to emulate.

One of Randall's colleagues at The Lilly Library, Josiah Q. Bennett, called attention to Randall's "incredible skills in locating books" in *The David A. Randall Retrospective Memorial Exhibition: Twenty Years' Acquisitions,*[11] and it is quite clear that his greatest contribution as Lilly Librarian was the development of the collection. However, other aspects of running the Library were not neglected. Books and manuscripts were catalogued, and catalogued well, and they were made available to Indiana University students and faculty and to an increasing number of scholars from throughout the United States and from abroad who journeyed to Bloomington to use the resources assembled there. Lectures in the Library and many excellent exhibitions, some with lavish catalogues, called attention to the Library, music recitals were offered, and hours were extended to include evenings.

An unusual example of "outreach" was Randall's long-term loan, in 1971, of one of The Lilly Library's two copies of the first edition of Sir Walter Raleigh's *History of the World* for display in the Tower of London. Randall had noticed, on a visit to the Tower, among all the authentic furnishings of the room in which Raleigh wrote his *History* while a prisoner, that the copy of the book displayed was a 13th edition, published 50 years after the author's death.

Another of Randall's innovations was the sale of duplicates from The Lilly Library's collection, the first sale by an institution of books of this magnitude since the Huntington sale over four decades earlier. The sale was held at the Parke-Bernet Galleries in New York on the evening of November 8, 1962, and 150 lots realized over $220,000. The "star" of the sale was Caxton's 1478 printing of Chaucer's *The Canterbury Tales*, and among other outstanding items were the 1494 edition of the Columbus letter published in Basel, Copernicus' *De Revolutionibus Orbium Coelestium*, the Doves Press Bible, Eliot's Indian Bible, Locke's *Essay Concerning Human Understanding*, the Nuremberg Chronicle, and Vespucci's *Mundus Novus*. In his "Foreword" to the sale catalogue, Indiana University President Elvis J. Stahr, Jr. said that

> It is hoped that the action of Indiana University in disposing of these duplicate books will serve to advance the art of book collecting. Many college and university libraries count great resources today because of the generosity of the book collector and the labor of the bookseller. This sale is a slight gesture of recompense to that noble fraternity.[12]

These words echo the well-known statement of Frank J. Hogan on the sale of his library[13] and no doubt reflect Dave Randall's philosophy as well.

Still another innovative program in which Randall was involved was The Lilly Library Fellowship Program, a training opportunity for rare book librarians established in 1960 by Indiana University's Director of Libraries Robert Miller and Associate Director Cecil K. Byrd with support from the Lilly Endowment of Indianapolis.[14] The program trained fourteen librarians in rare book work from 1961 through 1970. The staff of The Lilly Library took on the responsibility of providing training and experience for the Fellows in all aspects of rare book librarianship and a highlight of the year was a trip to rare book libraries, dealers, and private collectors in Chicago and on the East coast with Randall. While Randall's participation in the program was the most informal and least structured of all the instructors, it offered a unique introduction to the world of rare books that probably could not have been obtained in any other way.[15]

Dave Randall was a distinguished member of the Bibliographical Society of America, the Grolier Club with which he traveled to Europe in 1959 and to Italy in 1962, the University Club of New York, and the Caxton Club of Chicago, and in 1959 he received the Sigma Delta Chi "Leather Medal" for outstanding contribution by a faculty member to Indiana University. In 1975 he selected 241 books and manuscripts representative of acquisitions made by The Lilly Library during his tenure. Meant for an exhibition and catalogue to mark his retirement, it became a memorial exhibition when Randall died on May 25, 1975, just a month before that retirement was to take place.

On September 10, 1975, friends of Dave Randall met in Bloomington to pay tribute to one of the great bookmen of his time. A copy of the Coverdale Bible, the first printing of the complete Bible in English, was presented to The Lilly Library on behalf of his friends and the University by Randall's son Ronald and it was accepted by Dean of Libraries W. Carl Jackson. Indiana University's Chancellor Herman B Wells, longtime colleague and friend Michael Papantonio, and Ronald Randall spoke eloquently the evening of September 10, but perhaps Chancellor Wells gave voice to the thoughts that were in the minds of many that evening when he said:

> The founding and development of the Lilly Library were occurrences of unexcelled importance during my

administrative years with the University. Its beginning and its successful evolution are jewels without measure. It was and it is Dave Randall's work.

It was indeed a lucky day for Indiana University and for me when Dave Randall decided to direct this great enterprise at Indiana University.[16]

NOTES

[1] Randall, David A. *Dukedom Large Enough*. New York: Random House, 1969, p. 18.

[2] *Ibid.*, p. 20.

[3] *Ibid.*, p. 53.

[4] The story of this copy of the Gutenberg Bible, the Schuckburgh copy, is told in detail in *Dukedom Large Enough*, pages 110-129. To promote its sale, Randall produced a sumptuously bound scrapbook containing an account of the book's discovery, a detailed description of it, a census of known copies, press clippings, and photographs.

[5] Bennett Cerf, fledgling co-founder of Random House and its Modern Library, asked Randall to put together a collection of first editions of books in the Modern Library list as an advertising gimmick. As a reward Cerf sent Randall a complete set of the Modern Library books. A cash reward would have been more welcome at the time. Later Randall provided stories for Cerf's syndicated book column and Cerf commissioned Randall to write *Dukedom Large Enough*.

[6] Randall, David A. Letter to the Editor, *Antiquarian Bookman*, 38 (October 3, 1966): 1294.

[7] Copies of correspondence relating to the establishment of the *Bibliography of American Literature* will be found in the collection of Ronald R. Randall.

[8] Randall, *Dukedom*, p. 353.

[9]Randall was not a charter member of the Baker Street Irregulars, but he was an early member, invited to join by Christopher Morley who, with Edgar W. Smith, signed Randall's certificate of membership. He joined the group in time to attend the memorable meeting at which Rex Stout proved that Doctor Watson was a woman.

[10]*Printing and the Mind of Man: A Descriptive Catalogue Illustrating the Impact of Print on the Evolution of Western Civilization During Five Centuries.* Comp. and ed. by John Carter and Percy H. Muir. London: Cassell & Co., Ltd., 1967, p. xii.

[11]Bennett, Josiah Q. "The Exhibition" in *The David A. Randall Retrospective Memorial Exhibition: Twenty Years Acquisitions.* Bloomington: Indiana University, The Lilly Library, 1975, p. 8.

[12]Stahr, Elvis J., Jr. "Foreword" to *An Important Selection of Incunabula, Americana, Literary & Scientific Classics, Duplicates from the Lilly Library, Indiana University, Sold by Order of the Trustees.* . . . New York: Parke-Bernet Galleries, Inc., 1962, p. [v].

[13]Fleming, Robert V. "Foreword" to *American Literature, First Editions, Autograph Letters, Manuscripts...The Frank J. Hogan Library...Part One.* . . . New York: Parke-Bernet Galleries, Inc., 1945, p. [3].

[14]Byrd, Cecil K. "The Lilly Fellowship Program at Indiana University," *College & Research Libraries,* 27 (July, 1966): 287-290.

[15]Silver, Joel. "The Lilly Fellowship Program: Training for Rare Book Librarians," *Rare Books & Manuscripts Librarianship,* 5 (No. 1, 1990): 33-38.

[16]"Lilly Library Tributes to Dave Randall," *AB Bookman's Weekly,* 56 (November 10, 1972): 2118.

PART II

1

THE LEGION OF THE LOST (1931)

This charming essay on "lost books" was Randall's first major publication. [From The Colophon, A Book Collectors' Quarterly, 7 (September, 1931): 5-12.]

WHAT songs the sirens sang is a difficult problem, though we are told on competent authority that it is not beyond all hope of solution. But even in our wildest dreams we have never hoped to recover the unsung tales of love and languishment that passed with the breath of Keats, while the stories that died when suave Walpole ceased dallying with his ladies on Strawberry Hill long enough to emit the few blasts necessary to drive poor Chatterton to a suicide's grave do not even abide our question. They are sunk with the wars of Kubla Khan in those "caverns measureless to man" that hold the unwritten Canterbury Tales and Milton's untold Arthurian epic.

Though I have indulged myself in fancy in attempting to plumb their depths as often as most, for me there is greater anguish in recalling, not the books that have remained unwritten, but those that have been written and disappeared - the legion of the lost. Philosophically, I suppose, this bias is unsound. At least Aristotle argues somewhere, I recall, that the truly tragic must of necessity deal with what might have been rather than what merely has been. But Aristotle notwithstanding, I continue to cherish my bibliographical prejudices and maintain that lost books, those that have disappeared simply because no one even thought enough of them to preserve them, present a more tragical tale than the entire roster of the world's unwritten masterpieces.

And when I speak of "lost works" I do not mean the writings of the ancients. The loss, for example, of the polemical writings of two hundred authors whose very names are known to us only through Eusebius's casual reference to them in his ecclesiastical histories does not move me nearly. The lost plays of Euripides, however, are another matter; indeed one of the major tragedies of literature. And I mourn as much as the next the vanished libraries of Athens, Rome, Pergamus and Constantinople (which is reputed to have contained the only authentic copy of the proceedings of the Council of Nicea, together with the works of Homer written in letters of gold).

Perhaps the greatest literary holocaust on record is the tale of the destruction of the Alexandrian Library, which was founded by Ptolemy Soter, whose son purchased for it the library and manuscripts of Aristotle, all of which perished, together with some seven hundred thousand other volumes, at the orders of the Calif Omar. He reasoned that "if these writings of the Greeks agree with the Koran, or Book of God, they are useless and need not be preserved; if they disagree they are pernicious and ought to be destroyed," and forthwith proceeded to feed the fires of four thousand baths of the city with the pearls of the ages. Though Gibbon, with his usual prejudice for the Saracens, attempts to disprove the story, he really needn't have bothered, for the Calif Omar's logic was just as impeccable as that of the Christian cleric who accompanied Simon de Montfort to the land of the troubadours to slaughter the Albigensians and who, when the commander appealed to him during the storming of one of the cities as to what method should be used to spare the true believers, answered "Kill them all. God will know his own." It is as fruitless to weep for the slaughtered innocents killed in the resultant sack as it is to weep for the treasures burned in the baths of Alexandria. They are gone and beyond recall. It is the poems and plays and essays of our own English authors that have been printed, and bound, and sold, and have vanished, that I mourn, for, God willing, they may yet be found.

It is a sad fact, but it is true, that the mere circumstance of an author's having achieved print does not guarantee him a vicarious immortality, fondly as he may hope that it does. For fire and water, dust and damp, worms, rats, unkindly hands and pure neglect are but a few of the many "Enemies of Books" about whom Blades wrote so charmingly many years ago. The immense mortality rate is perhaps known fully only to the seasoned bibliophile. Between 1593 and 1636 were printed thirteen editions of Shakespeare's "Venus and Adonis." While we do not know with much certainty the size of the editions of the Elizabethan plays we may logically assume, on economic and other grounds (the usual retail price was two shillings sixpence, perhaps two dollars today), that they consisted of at least five hundred copies. And of these sixty-five hundred books issued over a period of forty-three years but twenty-one copies are known today despite the intense researches of nearly two hundred years. The first edition survives by but three examples, the second is totally lost, while of the third we have but two copies.

Pure accident seems responsible for the survival of many authors (the preservation of the single manuscript of Beowulf, incidentally, reads like a fairy tale), and the works remaining are not always those the authors would willingly have trusted to bear their reputations to posterity had they been consulted on the subject. William Grocyn, for example, was the guiding spirit of the flower of the early English philologists, the Oxford Humanists, and defended Aristotle with virtuous ardor. Today, and he must writhe in his grave to know it, he evades oblivion by but one slight and scarcely erudite composition. For Grocyn, companion of More the Lord Chancellor, of Colet the Dean of St. Paul's, of Linacre the great physician; Grocyn whom Erasmus termed "the friend and protector of us all" and whom Aldus the famous Venetian scholar and printer praised as "a man of exceeding skill and universal learning, even in Greek, not say Latin," greets posterity's avid readers with one charming epigram upon a lady who snowballed him!

Much of the work of that brilliant, bitter, irascible, satirical and lovable poet, Skelton, has been lost. His "Garlande of Laurell," "Sovereign Interlude of Virtue," and "Comedy of Achedemois" have survived only in title. Rigid suppression by his implacable enemy Cardinal Wolsey may account for their disappearance. We know that his most famous poem, "Colin Clout" - far from his best, but more widely known than the others chiefly because from it Spenser took his nom de plume - circulated for a long period only in manuscript because those at whom his vicious satire was aimed (Wolsey and his Hampton Court cabal)

Wyll nor suffre this book
By hoke ne by croke
Prynted for to be,"

and perhaps the above mentioned works perished in manuscript. But this assumption is somewhat invalidated by the fact that another play of his, "Nigramansir: A Moral Interlude and a Pithy," which is now lost (its charming title promises much), was known less than two centuries ago, for William Collins showed Thomas Warton a copy which has since vanished.

The knowledge of this episode has led me to the bottom of more than one bookstack I have been tempted to leave half examined. It is worthy of passing note, though, that suppression has accounted for the absolute disappearance of relatively few printed books, as human nature always treasures the forbidden; yet one example comes to mind, the "Liber Conformitatio" of the Franciscans, where censorship adequately accomplished the complete destruction of three entire editions.

How many English writers' works have not been fortunate to survive even by title is of course beyond conjecture. W. Wagner's "The Cruel Brother" is known only by one leaf, and John Bale's "Brief Comedy or Interlude of John Baptystes preaching in the Wilderness" is utterly untraceable. Scores of other early English works are known merely through a stray leaf or title-page and then only because "that wicked old biblioclast" John Bagehot tore an incredible number of them loose from their bindings to paste in huge scrapbooks preparatory to writing a history of English literature he never undertook. Shakespeare himself has not escaped, for it is well to remember that no copy of his "Love's Labour's Won" has ever been discovered (and it will be a sad day for those scholars who have written elaborate theses proving it never existed if it ever does turn up), and although we have every reason to believe his sonnets were in private circulation as early as 1595 - whether in manuscript or type is uncertain - they are now known only by the 1609 pirated edition.

The great fire of London in 1666 is commonly held to have destroyed great numbers of early printed books and probably it did, but sheer popularity is almost as dangerous as fire. The first translation (said to be by Samber) of Perrault's "Tales of Mother Goose (Contes de Ma Mère l'Oie)" is known only through a contemporary advertisement announcing its publication. It was probably literally read to pieces. Its sentimental and historical value may be indicated by recalling that in its pages the immortal Cinderella first appeared in our English tongue. But the saddest story is not of the best sellers whose immediate popularity caused the destruction of most of the earliest editions and which survive in countless reprints ("The Pilgrim's Progress" is a case in point), but in those works of which we have been writing which, caviar to the general, sank without a ripple into "the dark backward and abysm of time" - masterpieces for aught we know and to be recovered sometime, perhaps.

Dr. Johnson remarked on a memorable occasion that "Oliver Goldsmith was a man who, whatever he wrote, did it better than any other man could," and he repeated himself when he penned Goldsmith's epitaph, perhaps the loveliest in Westminster Abbey: "Nullum tetigit quod non ornavit." Remembering this, it is pitiful to recall that at least two of his works, translations of the "Life of Christ" and "The Lives of the Fathers," no longer exist. We have almost perfect assurance that he wrote them; the receipts paid him by Newbery the publisher are extant, and we are told that they were published in a "Christian magazine" edited by the infamous Parson Dodd and later reprinted in shilling pamphlets, but to date they have not been identified. They were probably published anonymously and were hack work, yet even hack work, when it is Goldsmith's, is not to be scorned. And it seems incredible that much of Blake's writings should have vanished, but it remains a fact that no less than ten are lost or conjectural. In his prospectus for October 10, 1793, he offered among other items "The History of England, a small book of Engravings, price 3s," and no one seems to have even purchased it, or preserved it if he did part with the necessary three shillings, for it is otherwise unknown. Crabb Robinson, writing in his diary and reminiscences, says: "He [Blake] showed me his Vision (for so it may be called) of Genesis 'as understood by a Christian visionary' in which in a style resembling the Bible the spirit is given. He read a passage at random. It was striking." And this is all we know of it - that it was "striking." Blake himself has written, "The Art [of fresco painting] has been lost; I have recovered it. How this was done will be told, together with the whole process, in a work of art now in press," and we are still awaiting Blake's revelation, for no copy or manuscript has survived.

And Shelley, too, has suffered. His "Leonora" was completely set up in type, that much is certain. Today not a single proof sheet, copy, or manuscript survives. His "Poem on a Fête at Carleton House" and "Essay on Love" (he mentioned the former in a letter dated January 16, 1812) have likewise disappeared. They will turn up, if they ever do (and your true bibliographer never quite despairs), in a pile of miscellaneous books priced fifty cents, or for that matter in a haystack. Systematic search for them is hopeless.

George Borrow has set many a collector chasing a phantom in the shape of his "Life and Adventures of Joseph Sell," or for that matter perhaps he hasn't. His wife declared the book a hoax and stated it was never printed, but one cannot be sure of anything but his genius when dealing with Borrow, and it is safer at times to be sceptical of that. It is a matter of record that his third literary venture, "Tales of the Wild and Wonderful," London, 1825, was unknown until 1921, when Mr. Walter Jerrold contributed an account of it to the *Cornhill Magazine*. Since then some half dozen copies have turned up, enough at any rate to change its status in the rare book catalogues from "hitherto unknown" to "extremely rare." It may someday turn out that Joseph Sell is not such (I restrain myself from the obvious pun with difficulty) a hoax as it now appears to be. And to close with a modern example: Did Robert Louis Stevenson write for a California magazine "The Surprise?" It has been stated that he did, but the truth is not known for the simple reason that no issue of the magazine, besides the first, has ever been discovered.

It is not impossible that all books here mentioned may be sometime recovered and made available through reprints to the student and collector. It is not impossible, I repeat, but I would rather, in case of bets, place my money upon the hopes of recovering the siren's song. The will o' the wisp does materialize on occasion, however. Richard Brinsley Sheridan's "Speech on the 7th of February in bringing forward the Fourth Charge against Warren Hastings, Esq., Relative to the Begums of Oude" was one of the most memorable ever delivered in Parliament. He spoke for five hours and when he stopped "the whole house - the members, the peers, the strangers - involuntarily joined in a tumult of applause, new and irregular in that house, by loudly and repeatedly clapping their hands," and Pitt hastily moved the adjournment of the debate on the grounds that the minds of the members were too agitated to discuss the matter coolly. So great was the impression that when Sheridan came to speak as the manager of the impeachment the following year seats sold readily for as much as fifty pounds a piece.

Iolo Williams, Sheridan's bibliographer, confessed himself unable to locate a copy of the printed speech and students for years ransacked London and its environs in vain search of it. Recently the writer discovered a copy by merest chance in a bundle of apparently worthless pamphlets in New York, but a short time after - mark this - a friend unearthed one in Philadelphia. Sheridan's speech which moved Parliament to the unwonted height of handclapping one hundred and forty-four years ago disappears utterly to appear twice in succession within a few weeks in these United States. Truly the path of Lost Books leads sometimes to the rainbow's end: And if the Gods are good and one attains to it and snatches from oblivion some part of this lost legion one can only fall reverently on one's knees. With Edmund Gosse, when after a particularly brilliant piece of literary detective work he discovered and definitely attributed to the pen of Matthew Arnold (who was loth to identify it) the hitherto unknown "Alaric at Rome," and fervently pray that no one ever discover another.

2

THE HOGAN SALE OF
AMERICAN LITERATURE (1944)

David Randall often wrote about collectors and their collections, usually from firsthand information. Here he describes the American books in Frank J. Hogan's collection that were to be auctioned early in 1945, with some insights into Hogan as a book collector and some comments on recent auctions. [From Publishers' Weekly, 146 (November 25, 1944): 2068-2070.]

WHEN Frank J. Hogan, of Washington, D.C. died last summer his will provided for the sale of his books at auction in New York as soon as was practicable after his death. "I had thought of bequeathing my valuable books and collection of autograph and literary manuscript material, including my collection of first and rare editions of English and American literature, to some institution to be permanently kept together as a collection, but this idea I have abandoned in favour of a plan that will accomplish their dispersion among those coming after me, who will experience, as I have felt, a profound happiness and satisfaction in possessing these precious monuments of human thought and progress. There is something sacred in the spiritual and intimate companionship of a book, and I do not deem it fitting that these friends of many happy hours should repose in unloved and soulless captivity. Rather, I would send them out into the world again to be the intimates of others, whose loving hands and understanding hearts will fill the place left vacant by my passing."

In an interesting codicil to the will, typical of the realism which Mr. Hogan displayed in both his professional and his collecting career, he further stated that: "The drastic changes which have occurred in our national economy due to war conditions require me to take into account the ever-narrowing opportunities for disposing of such material, and for that reason I do not wish my executors to be required to force the material upon a scanty and unwilling market." He then conferred upon his executors "full discretionary power to dispose of the material free of any limitations as to time" (though not as to method).

Now the past auction season or so and certainly the present one, so far, at least, has not been notable for high, or even moderate, prices fetched by the type of literary material Mr. Hogan collected. Certain types of books have sold well, true enough: French books (as witness the Crowninshield sale), classic literature (Kalbfleisch), color-plate books (suitable for breaking up by print dealers), and press books are examples. But the records show that literary material, especially English, and particularly the more valuable items, has been forced upon, as Mr. Hogan foresaw, "a scanty and unwilling market." One needs only to recall the Howard Sachs sale in February to confirm this. And certainly a $90,000 gross for the Drexel Institute literary collection (including $5 fetched for the family Bible of the generous donor of that collection, George Childs) could not have led to any dancing in the streets by that Institute's misguided board of directors. There is probably no time in the past twenty-five years, in our opinion, that that particular sale could have been scheduled with less advantage to everyone concerned.

However the Hogan executors have decided to sell a portion of his library in January. They have wisely selected, we believe, to offer first his notable collection of American books. Though by no means the major portion of his great library, either in numbers or value (the English literature from 1700 to the present is larger, the English literature before 1700 much more valuable), it is one he particularly loved and upon which he concentrated his interest in the last two or three years of his brief collecting career. And it is a collection which should bring forth much more competition than his comparable English books would at this time.

The sale will certainly offer for those wise enough to take advantage of it as fine a collection of American literature as has been sold at public auction in most of our collecting lifetimes and probably the finest ever offered in this century. It does not have the intensive concentration on New England authors that the Wakeman collection had, nor long lots of some early authors that Braislin possessed, but it has a catholicity these and other similar collections lacked. It ranges from the first American novel, "The Power of Sympathy," to a miniature copy of a translation into French of Steinbeck's "The Moon is Down" ("Nuit Sans Lune") dropped by the R.A.F. over occupied countries in 1942.

The collection of early American first editions of fiction is distinguished though not extensive. It includes Wharton's "The Coquette," Belknap's "The Forester's" (in original boards), Charlotte Rowson's "Charlotte," some Charles Brockden Browns, etc. There is a complete (we believe) collection of books listed in Merle Johnson's "High Spots," including Crane's "Maggie" and Harte's "M'liss" (both in wrappers), Hawthorne's "Fanshawe" and "Peter Parley's History," "The Last of the Mohicans," in boards, "The Sketch Book," in parts, etc. There is also the complete collections of books listed in Merle Johnson's "You Know These Lines," formed by him when compiling his bibliography, including the excessively rare Sarah J. Hale's "Poems for Our Children," containing "Mary Had a Little Lamb."

Mr. Hogan, with his charming Irish sentiment, loved "association items" and had some gorgeous ones: "Huckleberry Finn," inscribed to U.S. Grant, Jr.: "Sister Carrie," given by Dreiser to his brother; "Knickerbocker's History of New York," Irving's own copy, annotated; Sinclair's "The Jungle," inscribed by the author to Mark Twain; Hawthorne's "Gentle Boy," "House of Seven Gables" and "Twice-Told Tales" (both the 1837 and 1842 editions), given to members of his family; the famous copy of Cooper's "The Spy" (in boards) inscribed by him to Mrs. Banyer, John Jay's daughter, who started Cooper on his literary career. The Melvilles are remarkable, the finest ever offered at public sale, and include the dedication copy of "Mardi" and two source books for "Moby Dick," both with Melville's annotations.

Lest the collector of modern firsts think that Mr. Hogan collected only the "classic" Americans, here is a list of some of the books which are due in January, a goodly lot of which have either never appeared at public auction, or appeared very rarely: Hemingway's "For Whom the Bell Tolls" (one of 15 copies especially bound for the author's own use); Wolfe's "Look Homeward Angel" (advance copy in wrappers); Wilder's "The

Bridge of San Luis Rey" (one of 21 copies); Wylie, "Incidental Numbers" (her first book, virtually unknown and unobtainable). There are also practically complete collections of Dreiser, Hemingway, O. Henry, Lewis, etc.

We have left for the last, the Poes. There is nothing to be said of these that will not be said louder in the sale itself, but here will appear the finest collection of Poe ever offered at public auction. It is complete (except for the "Murders in the Rue Morgue") from "Tamerlane" on. There are Poe's own copies of "The Conchologist's First Book" and "Eureka"; "Al Aaraaf," inscribed by Poe's sister; "The Raven," with the manuscript of the last stanza in Poe's hand; the manuscripts of the first draft of "The Bells," of the "Domain of Arnheim," of "The Spectacles," and similar material.

It is to be hoped that American collectors of our literature will not neglect the finest opportunity to enrich their collections they are likely to have in many a decade. It is also to be hoped that should the ensuing literary auction season prove inconclusive the remainder of the Hogan collection will not be *forced* on a "scanty and unwilling market." If the market, through no fault of its own, can't at the moment absorb material of the highest quality it certainly shouldn't be "forced" to attempt what is bound to be disastrous.

3

THE SADLEIR COLLECTION (1953)

This dedicatory address is a pleasant blend of personal reflection on Michael Sadleir and his collection of Victorian fiction and some insights into the content and uses of the collection. [From *The Sadleir Collection: Addresses Delivered by Frederick B. Adams, Jr. and David A. Randall at the Dedication Ceremonies, University of California at Los Angeles Library, November 13, 1952.* Los Angeles: Friends of the UCLA Library, 1953, pp. 13-19.]

The London *Times Literary Supplement* of April 13, 1951, in reviewing the catalogue of the Michael Sadleir collection, commented that, "It is given to few book collectors to exert a decisive influence on the technique as well as on the taste of their age. . . It is one thing, and a very fine thing, to assemble a great collection in the classic tradition or in the prevailing manner. It is another thing, and a much rarer one, to change the whole climate of book collection." Yet that is exactly what Sadleir did.

And he was able to do this, to initiate a new approach to a fourth dimension in book collecting technique, largely because his background as publisher, editor, and author, gave him a knowledge of book structure, book distribution, and book production which other collectors lacked. It is very seldom indeed that all these qualities are found in one person.

For one thing, publishers are seldom antiquarians--they are forward looking people and have to be if they are going to stay in business and remain solvent. Publishing is, they say, "the worst business in the world," and its problems are never solved. I should know, I'm employed by a publishing firm myself. A half-century ago publishers were certain that the bicycle craze was corrupting youth to the point where everyone would grow up illiterate, if healthy, and publishing was doomed. A generation later it was automobiles and movies, non-talking. (On these at least you had to read captions.) Still later it was radio, then talking-pictures, and now television, all driving the nation into illiteracy and publishers into bankruptcy. This is one reason why publishers are not antiquarians. They are not interested in their past, from which they could learn a lot, mainly because they are so frightened of their future. Yet, Sadleir is a publisher, present head of the honored house of Constable, of London.

Editors are not antiquarians either--at least I never knew one who was; they are too concerned with next year's books to worry about past year's achievements. They have, as Scribner's editor, Burlingame, has put it, "to tease, cajole, humor, placate and scold angry and brooding men and women who have found a superfluous semicolon or refused to believe a royalty report, or searched the *Times* in vain for an advertisement or been unable to buy a copy of their precious book at a bookstore." It's a full-time job being an editor, you can't be a collector too. Yet Sadleir was again an exception. He could and did cope with Mary Webb, who took a lot of coping with, while simultaneously doing research on Trollope and Gothic fiction.

Nor does the novelist usually collect books. He is too busy trying to write them, and after a family and taxes he hasn't much left to collect books with. It was only a few years ago that Hawthorne, (Julian) said:

> I will engage to entertain at dinner, at a round table five feet in diameter, all the American novelists who make more than a thousand dollars a year out of the royalty of any one of their novels, and to give them all they want to eat and drink, and three of the best cigars apiece afterwards, and a hack to take them home in; and I will agree to forfeit a thousand dollars . . . if $25 does not liquidate the bill and leave enough over to buy a cloth copy of each of the works in question, with the author's autograph on the fly-leaf.

And times haven't changed much.

Yet publisher-editor Sadleir is also a contemporary novelist of notable success, as Mr. Adams has pointed out.

Again, scholars, generally are not collectors, though they are antiquarians. They are thorough examiners of the treasures others have accumulated but they seldom do the accumulating themselves, and they are capable, I understand, of driving librarians to the verges of various distraction by their insatiate demands for research material. But this is understandable because their job is interpretation, not accumulation. Yet here again, Sadleir is a scholar. His work in Victorian fiction was pioneer stuff, as witness his Trollopes, his work on Blessington-d'Orsay, a great success, and his work on Bulwer Lytton, a flat failure, yet the book, I think, nearest his heart. As Sadleir himself says a little ruefully, speaking both as author and publisher,

> It had been my intention to follow Bulwer with a second, and maybe a third book on the later phases of his pathetic, preposterous yet impressive career; but the plan was abandoned when it became clear that the reading public had no interest whatsoever either in Bulwer Lytton himself or his miserable marriage, or the papier-mache splendours of the high society of his day. The extent to which Bulwer flopped still astonishes me. Now and again I dip into it: and find all manner of ironies, absurdities and pathos, as well as glimpses of the life and shams of the period displayed or betrayed in contemporary periodicals and literature, which offer uneasy parallels to those of a few years ago. These elements of the book at least should, in my judgment as a publisher, have found their mark. But my judgment as a publisher was at fault. No one wanted Bulwer or ever pretended that he did.

There is no need for me to go into any detail on how or why Sadleir became a collector. This is told candidly and most entertainingly in his Preface to the two volumes, quarto, published in America last year by the University of California Press called *Passages from the Autobiography of a Bibliomaniac*. One learns here how, and why, he collected the books he did, the use he made of them and the lucky breaks he had - good book stories proving that virtue is rewarded. And proving again, despite the impressive evidence of Robert Browning to the contrary, that occasionally "the time and the place and the loved one" do come together. This resplendent collection could not have been brought together at any other time, nor by any other person.

Sadleir collected, as Mr. Adams pointed out, at an ebb tide. When he became interested in the period, Lytton Strachey and his acidulous pen caused the term "Victorian" to have a farcical and smug connotation, part of which it retains even now.

Commentators of the time forgot, if they ever knew, that Victorian fiction was not exclusively stories of haughty nobility and ruined maidens. It was also a magnificent period of novel writing aside from the silver fork school - of great and courageous novels of social protest by Frances Trollope, Disraeli, Mrs. Gaskell, Charles Kingsley, Gissing, and others; of political novels, such as W. H. Mallock's forgotten *The New Republic, or Culture, Faith and Philosophy in an English Country House* - (a very full title indeed, but a brilliant novel in which you will find Walter Pater, Jowett, Ruskin, Arnold, and Huxley debating every aspect of contemporary life and philosophy), and Disraeli's little read *Endymion*; as well as novels of manners, adventure, the sea, religion, sport, and so on.

Sadleir was never one of the intelligentsia who branded the Victorians as merely snobbish materialists. He knew better; he had read their novels. And speaking of reading novels, there still prevails the absurd notion that Victorian fiction is abysmally long. That it takes one three snowed-in-winter months in the high Sierras to finish one book. When a monstrous book came out of Texas last month, in two volumes, about 800,000 words, the reviews I saw all equated it with Victorian fiction, i.e. three-deckers, and lamented that while a hundred years ago in a more gracious, and duller, age people may have had time for such prolonged reading, we don't.

This again is just not so. The physical format of the three-decker was imposed by publishing convention and necessity and resisted change till the 1880's. The books were meant to be lent, not sold. They cost new 31/6, the equivalent of at least $25.00 today. And that explains, in part, their rarity. But they were not long. On an average, each volume contained fewer than 50,000 words - 150,000 for the three, considerably less than the average novel today. The really long novels, *Pickwick* and *Vanity Fair*, came out in parts - serialized - over a two-year period, and were not intended to be taken in one gulp, any more than are martinis.

In many respects, Sadleir knows better than most, the three-decker format militated against some types of creative writing. Rhoda Broughton, author of *Cometh Up as a Flower*, was a sufferer from this publishing convention. As Sadleir says in his notable essay on her in his recent *Things Past*, she had to submit to this tyranny for purely financial reasons, and though her earlier novels " . . . horrified censorious mid-Victorians and anonymous reviewers, they were eagerly devoured by those whom the moralists claimed to protect and the reviewers to influence." Her emancipation from this straight-jacket came too late to do her much good.

The first time I met Michael Sadleir was in 1934 when he was visiting his "opposite number" in America, the late Carroll Atwood Wilson. My wife and I were living at the time on 10th Street just off 4th Avenue in New York, then as now the center of the second-hand bookshops, whose contents Sadleir eagerly pillaged. But it was also then, as alas it no longer is, the center of another great American culture - killed in our town by our late mayor "the little flower," La Guardia - the burlesque shows, notably at Irving Place. Sadleir was enchanted with all this and could conceive of no happier spot outside London. He had his choice of three burlesques and at least thirty second-hand bookshops in a three-block radius. "All this and heaven too!" Sadleir, by the way, as readers of *Fanny by Gaslight* must know, is England's accepted authority on London night-life of a few generations ago.

How this fascinating collection was formed is reasonably well documented, but I would like to reinforce Mr. Adams' opinion of the sheer physical perfection of the books themselves.

Nowhere in the British Isles can be seen now, as they were issued, these lovely volumes - and if you want a contrast in just good bookmaking, look at the dowdy first American edition of *Moby Dick* and compare it with that splendid three-volume Bentley *The Whale* - the publisher's own copy. This is a point Sadleir makes clear in his Autobiography where he says (italics are his) he learned to love the Victorian novel *"as a physical thing."* I hope that another few generations from now these books will still be as they are, otherwise the then librarian will look up some night and say "Speak, speak, thou fearful guest . . . Why dost thou haunt me?" I do not mean to imply, nor would Sadleir, that this is a collection of *objet d'art*; it is a working library of enormous scholarly value, and should be used as such, but used carefully and gratefully.

Just a few ending words on how this collection came across three thousand miles of water and three thousand miles of land, to rest permanently at UCLA.

Well, I am addressing the "Friends of UCLA" and I would like to tell you that you have more friends than you know of. When Sadleir decided to dispose of these books the problem was placed before my Scribner colleague in London, John Carter. It was obvious from the start that the collection should not be broken up. Too much time and intelligence and effort had gone into its forming to even consider that. Among several universities interested, the problem of duplication raised, as usual, its ugly head. So, one way and another, things hung fire. Until, just about ten months ago, I received a phone call from Dr. Powell. Was the Sadleir Collection still on the market? It was. Could it be bought for a named sum? Of this I was doubtful (dealers and librarians seldom see eye to eye on such trivial details). And finally, could I find some outside encouragement to back up his opinion about the collection's value, like, for instance, an appraisal by a competitor? And, this all had to be right away, not just next week; yesterday would have been preferable.

This was a very large order on very short notice and I remember asking Powell on the phone if he had holes in his head. As it happened, there was a meeting that afternoon of a committee, of which I am a member, of the Bibliographical Society of America, dealing with an enormous projected bibliography of American literature, and I told, partly jokingly, of Larry's call to me. Immediately everyone present, including Mr. Adams and James Babb, Librarian of Yale, agreed that this collection should come to America, and come, also, to UCLA. And they wired everyone so; Dr. Bradford Booth (who needed no urging), Dr. Powell, and others. So ended a pleasant day's work, I thought.

But there was Larry on the phone next morning. The trouble was, it seemed, that the amiable Messrs. Adams, Babb, et al, though enthusiastic about the Sadleir collection, and estimating correctly its quantity and quality and value, both commercial and to scholarship, had never actually at that time physically examined the books themselves. Could I get another endorsement from someone who had? There are times, I think, I ought to go back to the Pennsylvania coal mines I came from. John L. Lewis has fewer problems - but less fun, also.

Well, there was one such person, Dr. Gordon Ray of the University of Illinois, which also had a library, and was also avid to purchase the Sadleir collection and was only waiting their next financial budget to do so. Furthermore, Dr. Ray had just recently been to England and spent considerable time going over these books with an eye to eventual purchase. An appeal to him brought a prompt and most generous reply. "Illinois wants this, of course, but we are unable to close now so let's by all means get it to America and, specifically to UCLA." This demonstration of friendliness, of cooperation in bringing here the raw materials of scholarship, and the sacrifice of one's own hopes, seems to me to be an impressive example of the kind of unity we need.

A few months ago the legislature of another state decided, I am told, that certain state funds could not be used for the purchase of books, because books were not "permanent improvements." I find it difficult to conceive of anything more absurd. Certainly UCLA has acquired a permanent improvement in the Sadleir collection and I, for one, won't live long enough to read the fruitful works its possession will inspire.

It was therefore by no accident, as I hope to have made clear, that Michael Sadleir gathered these 8,500 odd volumes, nor was it by any accident that your librarian acquired them. UCLA has something functional, not merely decorative, and buds are already shooting out. It is a great collection, and it will grow.

4

JOSIAH KIRBY LILLY (1957)

Shortly after J. K. Lilly presented his great library to Indiana University, David Randall published this history of its formation and summary of its contents as number fourteen in the "Contemporary Collectors" series in "The Book Collector." [From The Book Collector, 6 (Autumn, 1957): 263-277.]

When I was invited by *The Book Collector* to write an account of the library formed by J. K. Lilly, of Indianapolis, and recently given by him to Indiana University, at Bloomington, I realized at once that it would be impossible to convey any adequate idea of the quantity, variety, quality and importance of Mr. Lilly's achievement 'within an upper limit of 6000 words'. Indeed, a mere listing of the more important books would overrun this limit; and few things are more boring than a list of titles--unless they are for sale.

Yet one does not simply say: 'Here is a superb library, one of the greatest ever assembled by a private collector', or that it is 'beyond question the most valuable and most extensive ever given to an American university', without documentation, and expect one's word to be taken for granted. Too many 'world renowned libraries', known by reputation only, have failed to win the world's renown when placed on public exhibition. And 6000 words would be inadequate in this case even to introduce many of the categories of book collecting in which the library's founder interested himself.

These valid objections were overridden by the amiable autocrat of the editorial board with the suggestion that such an account 'might begin by answering the questions when, why, where, how, and what Mr. Lilly collected. This could lead on to something about the evolution of his tastes and interests; his principal sources of supply; his collecting methods; the limitations of the library, and so on. This, at the same time, seemed a simple enough request.

Mr. Lilly's collecting began in 1926 and the first order from a rare-book catalogue, which his secretary, Miss Armington--who is still with him--remembers, was for a minor item of Mark Twain's from James F. Drake, Inc. Later he ordered, among many others from the same firm, what was then the only and still remains the finest, presentation copy of *The Adventures of Tom Sawyer* (All titles mentioned, unless otherwise specified, are first editions). So much for the *When*.

As for the *Why*, that remains, as always in all collecting, elusive and generally unanswerable, and the writer of this article resolutely refuses to speculate. It suffices to say that Mr. Lilly comes from the most literate state in the USA, and is a born collector, from a collecting family.

Where he collected is, I believe, a feature unique in the formation of the few comparable American libraries, for the answer is: 'Right in his own back yard'. The library contains at the most only a scattered handful of books he personally bought abroad or ordered from foreign catalogues. The only exception coming to mind is the fine Americana, mostly early travels, bought from Henry Stevens, Son and Stiles of London--but even these were bought through Roland Tree and in America. No books, to my knowledge, were ever bought by Mr. Lilly on the Continent, not in his thirty years of collecting has he ever placed a single bid, directly or indirectly at Sotheby's or any of the other English or Continental auction houses--and precious few at American auctions, after the Kern sale! This came about, legend and *Book Auction Records* state, in 1929 at a time when he was just really getting started and his enthusiasm was high. He had been collecting along the general line of the usual American beginner of the period: the books on the Grolier and the A. Edward Newton 'Hundred' lists with (aside from his always present interest in the American scene) those English authors of the 19th and 20th centuries then so ardently sought after--Stevenson, Barrie, Moore, Kipling and the poets. He missed, luckily, getting involved in the then fashionable 18th century, but his targets were otherwise conventional.

But the competition was stiff. As he recalled later, there he was, a little book collector whom no one had ever heard of, from the midwest, just trying to buy a book in the Big City. He picked what he liked in the first session, bid the estimated limit, and didn't get a thing. At the second session he increased the estimates by fifty per cent; at the third session he doubled them--and still got nothing. And then, in what he concedes to have been a mistake, he concluded that his midwest money was just as good as that of the Wall Street boys and 'took the lid off'. One result is that the library now contains some very nice books from the latter part of the Kern sale. Others are that he seldom bid at auction from that time on and when he did, even when angling for such items as *The Bay Psalm Book*, he never gave an unlimited bid. As a collector he may have learned the hard way, but he learned fast and the lesson stuck.

Not that the collection does not contain a great many volumes which have passed through the notable libraries dispersed at auction during the past quarter of a century. The Ashburnham-Gilbey set of the first five editions of Walton's *Angler* (all in their original bindings, and including the only presentation copy known to me) comes to mind, with the Frank Hogan copy of the Caxton *Chaucer*, the Harmsworth *Milk for Babes*, Horace Walpole's copy of Howard's *Songes and Sonnettes*, 1559, from the Holford sale, among many others. He invariably knew of their forthcoming appearance at an auction, and as events proved he got them, although he did not go into direct auction competition for them. He let them be bought for stock by dealers who believed in them, and then purchased them from the dealer, never begrudging any profit which seemed fair--or even handsome.

This leads to the fourth question: *How?* The answer has been partially given--through American dealers, and a lot of them. Although the majority of the major items in the collection were obtained from relatively few and well-known sources, there are few rare-book specialists who have not sold to him directly, and none, I suspect, indirectly. All through his still continuing collecting career (we may add here that though his books are the apple of his eye, they are very, very far from being the alpha and omega of his collecting), he has been an extremely active member and director of one of America's largest businesses. Some system had to be evolved whereby the books he wanted came flowing into Eagle Crest Library, the Eli Lilly firm remained solvent, and he did his job. He simply could not spend the time necessary to read all catalogues (a full-time job for a professional librarian, as I am finding out), to carry out all the necessary correspondence, etc.; and he has never employed a librarian.

Gradually his collecting interests, along with his professional responsibilities, increased. The lure of American and English literature along the classic lines of the late 1920s and '30s, though it never exactly palled, was not enough to satisfy him and he therefore became interested in the possibilities of collecting the outstanding first editions of western European literature. In this he was stimulated, I like to think, by the pioneering catalogues which the more forward-thinking dealers, such as Elkin Mathews and Scribner, were issuing. His original interest (stemming from his service in France in World War I) was in 19th-century French literature. This led, eventually, to a collection of 'firsts' unique in the United States as regards original condition.

Mr. Lilly has always, and in all his collecting, insisted upon original condition wherever possible, and it is one of the things which make his library and accomplishment difficult to conceive without actual 'viewing'. The proportion of rebound copies to those in original state (I am referring now to the real rarities) is very low, and it should be added that Mr. Lilly himself has never had a volume rebound. A very hearty number of books, and some obvious titles, are lacking simply because they have not turned up in acceptable condition. Mention may be made in passing (as I may seem to have disparaged the 18th century), that his *Spectator*, Pope's *Essay on Criticism, Rape of the Lock*, and the four parts of the *Essay on Man*, as well as Gay's *Beggar's Opera* and *Polly*, are all in original state, uncut, as issued; so, too, are Burn's Kilmarnock *Poems* and the *Scot's Musical Museum*, the principal 18th-century quartos, etc.; and when a difficult book like *Moll Flanders, Pamela* or *Gulliver* could not be obtained thus, it had to be in original calf, and in the case of *Gulliver*, on small paper with the first state of the portrait.

This predilection for original condition carried over into the Continental 'firsts' and here Mr. Lilly's tastes remained his own. He wanted his favourite books, wherever possible, to be in their original state, 'wrappers, uncut, as issued', or, failing this, in a harmonious contemporary binding, and would have no truck with fine bindings for their own sake. Montaigne's *Essaies*, Racine's *Iphigénie*, Corneille's *Polyeucte*, are not uncut, though all are in original bindings, but in 19th-century literature, *Madame Bovary, La Peau De Chagrin, Les Trois Mousquetaires, Les Travailleurs de la Mer, L'Homme qui Rit,* most of Anatole France, Baudelaire, Zola on through *Jean-Christophe* and Proust's *Recherche* are in their original wrappers, uncut, as are Heine's *Gedichte* and *Buch der Lieder*. Few libraries in America or elsewhere, public or private, can boast of the first printing of Dostoievsky's *Crime and Punishment* and *The Brothers Karamazov*, as well as Tolstoy's *War and Peace*, fine Turgenievs, and other Russian novels, or *Pan Michael* and *Quo Vadis* and representative collections of the Scandinavian poets, philosophers, novelists and dramatists, in their original languages.

Having decided to extend the range of his collecting to comprehend all Western literature the next desideratum was some sort of guide-post which would summarize, to paraphrase Matthew Arnold, 'the best that has been thought and printed in the world.' This turned out to be a volume on his own reference shelves--Asa Don Dickinson's *One Thousand Best Books*. Purchases were not confined to this list by any means, but if a book which was on the list became available it was acquired in its original language and often in its first English translation as well. The Classics were also acquired in their first editions, in both Greek and Latin.

Once sights had been set, Mr. Lilly normally enlisted the aid of some trustworthy specialist in the field and then, within limits, turned him loose. 'Within limits' meant that books might be reported as found but would not be purchased until they had been seen by Mr. Lilly, whose exacting standards rejected a large proportion of those offered for inspection. All sections of the Library would have been much enlarged had these standards been relaxed. Although a strict yearly budget was adhered to, it was fortunately seldom that a book was turned down on account of its price.

Business interests naturally inclined him to collect medical and scientific books and at the start these were acquired as a chance dictated. But there came a time when he decided to set about the building of a really substantial collection in these related fields and again some guide-posts were needed. None, suitable for the purpose, appeared to exist. To be sure, there had been plenty of writing about medical books, and there were always Garrison and Osler to consult; but there was no satisfactory list, ranging from incunabula to Fleming, of the epoch-making discoveries in medicine and surgery and their first appearances in print. So, characteristically, Mr. Lilly had one prepared by W.R. LeFanu, Librarian of the Royal College of Surgeons of England. The same lack existed in Science and it was filled by I. Bernard Cohen, editor of *Isis*. These lists will eventually be published. Similar lists were also prepared, before Lyle Wright's well-known *American Fiction, 1774-1850*, appeared in print, by two American dealers, both specialists in this sphere--John S. Van E. Kohn and Howard Mott--whose subsequent sleuthing proved to be eminently successful.

While booksellers were reporting on various interests, Mr. Lilly was himself actively buying through catalogues and correspondence and on his numerous trips around the country, during which he became acquainted with many dealers. All this was done very quietly and with no publicity--not even that of lending books to exhibitions. People could come to see his treasures and be royally entertained, but once the rule of 'no lending to exhibitions' had been made it was not broken for anyone. As a result the collection has been little known until recently. Indeed, many of the dealers who supplied books in one subject had no idea of his interests in other subjects. A many-sided and very experienced collector, he once remarked to me wryly that he had a distaste for 'those dealers who expect to learn their business at my expense.'

The Lilly Library was thus to acquire a distinction which sets it apart from all others of its class formed in America. There were few 'bulk purchases'. Unlike Huntington with his acquisition of the Church Library, or Morgan with his purchases of entire collections, Mr. Lilly has collected almost all his books individually. They give, therefore, a much clearer picture of the founder's desires, aims and accomplishments.

His distaste for bulk purchases may best be illustrated by one incident. Just before 1939 he was offered what was claimed to be a complete collection of the works of Nobel Prize winners, in original state and in their original languages. It presented some tricky bibliographical problems because it included offprints from scientific journals and other unusual 'first appearances'. Mr. Lilly turned down the collection (though not the idea) with the remark: 'Let's not buy this, but go after them individually and have the fun of getting them ourselves.' And so, indeed, he did and thus secured in due course the majority of them.

The only exception to this rule, aside from such local interests as the James Whitcomb Riley and General Lew Wallace papers, was made in favour of early Americana. Although the Library was already strong in New England rarities, such as the Eliot *Indian Bible* (both editions in original bindings, the second a presentation), some twenty Cambridge (Mass.) imprints before 1700, and the like (mostly purchased from Goodspeed of Boston, or Dr. Rosenbach), no special attention had been paid to American beginnings, early discovery and exploration, as he felt that he had come too late into this field to gather a really distinguished collection. The lack of such material, and a realization of its importance, spurred by a reading of Kenneth Roberts's historical novels, tempted him when the outstanding collection of Baron Hardt was offered. Two Columbus letters, including *'Harisse* No. I', among a choice lot of about two hundred and fifty books, simply could not be turned down. (He once remarked to me about his Poe collection--the first important rarity he ever purchased was the romantic copy of *Tamerlane*, graphically described by Charles Goodspeed in his *Yankee Bookseller*--'there is nothing like beginning at the top and working down'.)

A word now about 'the limitations of the library' and some notes on its lesser known resources. Mr. Lilly's interests were never directed to early printing as such. His incunabula were acquired to support other interests: literature, science and exploration, books which influenced thought, etc. He was not attracted to the graphic arts, or to mediaeval texts, illuminated manuscripts, imprints, or fine bindings--though, having decided that the Library needed one example of a Grolier, he obtained one of the finest extant. This was the copy of Heliodorus, *Aethiopicae Historiae* used by William Loring Andrews as frontispiece to his book on Grolier, of which he wrote: 'The decoration is elaborate and beautiful in the extreme and it is undeniably one of the finest examples in existence, not excepting those in the great Paris libraries.' The incunabula include: Aristotle, *Ethica* (Strassburg c.

1469); Thomas à Kempis, *De Imitatione Christi* (with the slip; Augsburg c. 1470); Cicero, *Orationes* (Rome 1471); Herodotus, *Historiae* (Venice 1474); Bede, *Historia Ecclesiastica* (Strassburg c. 1475); Marco Polo, *Travels* (1st Latin); Homer, *Opera* (Florence 1488); *Suetonius*, (Venice 1490); and Aristophanes, *Comediae* (Venice 1498). There is not a Gutenberg Bible or a *Poliphilus*, the great alpha and omega of 15th-century printing, just as there are no Blakes from a later century; and the only example of 'press books' is a complete set--an early purchase--of Kelmscotts.

Only five of the Grolier Club's 'Hundred' are at present lacking in any shape or form, though it is hoped to reduce this number shortly to three. They are: Malory's *Le Morte D'Arthur*, Caxton, 1483; *The Booke of the Common Praier*, 1549; the King James Bible, 1611; Taylor's *Holy Living*, 1650, and Bunyan's *Pilgrim's Progress*, 1667. A few of the rarest of the ninety-five titles already in the Library are, however, either imperfect or are of the earliest edition available after the first. These include the Hogan copy of Caxton's *Canterbury Tales*, first edition but incomplete; Howard's *Songes and Sonnettes* (only the Bodleian copy of the first edition of 1557 is known), which is the 1559 edition but redeemed by being Horace Walpole's copy and unquestionably the most valuable book from his notable library; Lyly's *Euphues*, 1581, the fifth edition, one of three known copies, and heading a long run of his works; and Bacon's *Essaies*, 1598, the second edition, which is bound with Lord Cornwallis's *Essays*, 1600, in contemporary vellum. The rest are bibliographically correct and generally in acceptable condition by the most rigid standards, and a number are outstanding. Among these are: *The Rubaiyat* in original wrappers and inscribed to Max Muller; the Kilmarnock *Poems*, in original boards, uncut; Paine's *Rights of Man* with the correct imprint; the copy of *Evangeline* which Longfellow gave Hawthorne (who told him the story), and which heads a staggering array of presentation copies of this title; Hakluyt's *Principal Navigations*, 1598, with the first state of the Molyneux-Wright map; the Roxburghe-Devonshire-Clawson copy of the Caxton *Confessio Amantis*, bound by Hering; the correct first issue of Mrs. Browning's *Poems*, 1850, one of the very rarest books of 19th-century poetry; and superlative copies, all in original state, of Spenser, Donne, Milton, Herrick, Herbert, and many others. The four Shakespeare Folios are the John Rylands duplicates.

Some years ago Princeton University published in its *Biblia* (Feb. 1936) a list of 'The [*sic*] Hundred Great English Books'. (The Grolier Club more modestly entitled its list (1903) 'One Hundred Books Famous in English Literature,' and A. Edward Newton claimed only of *his* Hundred that they were 'Good Novels'.) A score-card was tabulated for the holdings of some of the leading American libraries which (in the Spring of 1955) credited the Huntington with 95; Yale with 92; Harvard with 83; Princeton with 76; and Chapin (Williams) with 72. The Lilly Library has a total of 87, which can be considered pretty good going for a private collector in the course of twenty-five years. And exactly the same percentage holds true of his holdings of the Grolier Club's *One Hundred Influential American Books Printed before 1900* (1947).

Ninety-nine of the Newton 'Hundred' are present, the single absentee being the 1865 *Alice in Wonderland*. Among the more notable titles in this group are the dedication copy of Galsworthy's *The Man of Property* (along with the Edward Garnett Galsworthy collection which includes some hundreds of autograph letters); presentations (always contemporary) of *Huckleberry Finn, The Red Badge of Courage, The Scarlet Letter; The Little Minister* (to Hardy), and others.

Manuscripts include *The Old Wives' Tale, Parnassus on Wheels,* and *Ben Hur. The Cloister and the Hearth* is in its presentation binding, inscribed to the author's mother. First editions of *East Lynne, Jane Eyre, Wuthering Heights* (complete with the elusive *Agnes Grey*), *Lady Audley's Secret, The Moonstone, Robbery under Arms,* and *Thaddeus of Warsaw* are all present in fine original state, as are also both the English and the American editions of *Moby Dick*, which appeared first in England, and *Ten Thousand A-Year*, which appeared first in America.

Some other remarkable copies are: *The Castle of Otranto*, presented, and with the author's autograph corrections; *Vathek*, Lausanne, 1786, one of two recorded copies in wrappers, uncut; *Marmion*, one of two copies recorded with the uncancelled leaves; Mrs. Gaskell's copy of the Aylott and Jones issue of the Bronte *Poems*; presentation copies of *The Revolt of Islam* and *Prometheus Unbound* to Edward Trelawney; a very superior collection of Gilbert and Sullivan; Hardy's *Dynasts*, presentations, including the 1903 Volume I and the much rarer 1905 Volume II; one of two advance copies of Synge's *Playboy*; one of three copies of the trial issue of Kipling's *Letters of Marque, Number One* (from a collection of hundreds of Kiplings); the copyright edition of Barrie's *The Wedding Guest* and a fine *Richard Savage*, from a Barrie collection surpassing the Kipling one.

A field of specialization, which can be only briefly covered here, is that devoted to books which have influenced thought. Some idea of the extent of this section of the Library may be gained by reference to a recent book by Robert Downs, Librarian of the University of Illinois, entitled *Books that Changed the World*, 'ranging' [according to the blurb] 'from Copernicus and Harriet Beecher Stowe to Darwin, Freud and Einstein'. All but one are present in first edition. Copernicus's *De Revolutionibus* has both states of the title-page (with and without errata); *Uncle Tom's Cabin* is represented by its original serial appearance in *The National Era* newspaper, edited by Whittier, as well as by all its appearances in book form; *The Origin of Species* is in book form, of course, but there is also Darwin's original paper with Wallace in printed wrappers as issued, on *The Tendency of Species to Form Varieties*, of which only one other copy (Harvard) is recorded. Other important works include Pope Gregory's *Kalendarium*; Rousseau's *Du Contrat Social* (first issue, thick paper, both states of the notorious cancelled leaf); Lenin's [*Factory Laws*]; Marx's *Das Kapital* (though not, alas, the *Communist Manifesto*); and so on through Roosevelt's *Looking Forward* (one of the few copies with uncorrected text).

Another of Mr. Lilly's special interests has always been juvenile literature and the Library is very rich in English, American and Continental firsts. Nineteenth-century American juveniles lead off with the first edition of Parson Weem's *Life of Washington*, one of only two copies known. The classic guide to this period is Jacob Blanck's *Peter Parley to Penrod*, and though it might be difficult to prove that here is the finest collection of these works ever assembled, it would be equally difficult to prove that it isn't. Suffice it to say that it contains Goodrich's *Tales of Peter Parley about America*, unique when acquired.

The first book Mr. Lilly remembers--it was read aloud to him by his mother--is Wyss's classic, familiarly known as *The Swiss Family Robinson*, and it is fully represented here, with its first appearance in magazine form; the first edition, *Der Schweizersche Robinson*, Zurich, 1812-1815; the first French translation by Mme

de Montolieu; and the first American printing.   Among other
Continental rarities are Grimm's *Kinder-und-Haus-Marchen* in
contemporary boards, and Hans Christian Andersen's *Eventyr*
(Series I and II), and *Nue Eventyr* (Series I-III); while the English
juveniles range from Thomas Day's *Sandford and Merton* through
Black Beauty (in the correct binding) to a nice set of Beatrix
Potters.

Special mention must be made of a group of four books
which can be found, side by side, in no other library in the world.
No other library, as a matter of fact, has even three of them; and
only six libraries (Congress, Yale, American Antiquarian Society,
Harvard, New York Public and the British Museum) can boast two.
In 1641 Thomas Shepheard published in London his *The Sincere
Convert*, three other copies only are recorded by Wing--Harvard,
British Museum and Congregational Library, London.   In 1646,
John Cotton published in London his *Milk for Babes, Drawn Out
of the Breasts of Both Testaments*, of which the Harmsworth-Lilly
and the British Museum copies are the only perfect ones known.
The Sincere Convert was translated into the Indian tongue by John
Eliot and printed at Cambridge, Mass., in 1689, and the *Spiritual
Milk for Boston Babes* (as it was re-titled), was likewise translated
and printed at Cambridge in 1691.   Of the six copies of each
recorded, the Lilly copies are certainly the finest, being bound
together in original sheep and in perfect condition.

Autographs were not sought with quite the persistence which
went into collecting of printed books, though there are some very
fine ones, including specimens of William Penn, George Rogers
Clark, Lord Amherst, Washington, Lincoln, etc.   Some of the
literary manuscripts have been mentioned; others include the
original manuscript of Barrie's *Peter Pan*, given by him to Maude
Adams, before it had a title (it is headed 'Anon,' and differs greatly
from the final version).   There is also the earliest known version of
Burns's *Auld Lang Syne* and the probably first draft of the *Address
of Robert Bruce to His Army before Bannockburn* and *O My Luv's
Like the Red, Red Rose*.   There are also splendid Keats and
Shelley and Emily Dickinson letters, among others of the 19th-
century poets.

Mr. Lilly's business naturally inclined him to acquire important
medical books and his collection of them is one of the finest ever
made by an individual anywhere.   He wanted the key works, the

first discoveries, whenever and wherever printed, and he in great part succeeded. The emphasis, as usual, was on significance, not value, and a five dollar book found a place on his shelves as readily as a five figure book if its contents justified its being there.

As this is a highly specialized field, there is no point in listing a long string of titles, though some indication of the Library's holdings may be given by mentioning Vesalius's *Fabrica* (both Basel, 1543 and 1555); Gemini's *Anatomie*, London, 1545 (STC listing only the BM and Bodleian copies); Harvey's *De Motu Cordis*, fine in original binding; and so on through the tragic *Die Aetiologie* of Semmelweiss, Rontgen, Pavlov, extensive Oslers, to Fleming, Banting and Salk. A majestic array indeed.

The same concentration holds true of science, with the same rigid adherence to quality. Copernicus's *De Revolutionibus* has already been mentioned. Kepler's *Astronomia Nova*, Prague, 1609, is an association copy; Bacon's *Instauratio* is large paper, original vellum, with his boar's head crest on the covers; Newton's *Principia* is in both states. The classics of mathematics, chemistry, geology, physics, etc., down to Smyth's account of the atom bomb are all well represented.

The American scene was Mr. Lilly's first love and his topographical collection is a major accomplishment. It must be dealt with all too briefly in my remaining space.

Books relating to Western exploration and conquest in general form an exciting though relatively small portion of the Library. Among the rarer early books not so far mentioned are *Harrisse* No. 4, the undated edition of the Columbus *Letter*; Enciso's *Suma de Geografia*, Seville, 1519; the complete nine Las Casas *Tracts*, 1552-1553; that great rarity, Alfonce's *Voyages Avantureux*, Poitiers, 1559; Gomara's *Historia . . . Mexico . . . Peru*, Caragoca, 1553, as well as the first Dutch (1554) and Paris (1569) editions. A special interest in Florida stemmed from the fact that Mr. Lilly spent many summers there as a boy and the collection ranges from the earliest discoveries to Romans' *Concise Florida*, New York, 1775.

Later summers spent on Cape Cod influenced his collecting of the earliest Americana, which range from the *Brief Relation*, London, 1622, through Roger William's *Key . . . Indian Language*, London 1643, to John Eliot's *Indian Tracts*, London, 1643-71 (the Church copies), and Hubbard's *Narrative*, Boston, 1677-86, in original binding, with the first state of the map (the Hawthorne family copy).

Early Virginiana include Hamor's *True Discourse*, London, 1615, first issue totally uncut, with a broadside proclamation of the Virginia Company used as wrappers; Captain John Smith's *Map of Virginia*, Oxford, 1612, the Bridgewater copy, and beautiful copies of his *Generall Historie*, the 1624 (with the rare portraits), 1627 and 1630 editions.

The Canadian collection is very choice and 17th-century items include, in the Lescarbot collection, the *Relation Derniere*, Paris, 1612; Champlain's *Voyages*, Paris, 1613, in original vellum with the map, as well as the 1619, 1620 and 1632 editions; and a beautiful set of thirty-three *Jesuit Relations*, Paris, 1635-1671--a score which would have been higher had there not been a commendable insistence upon original vellum bindings. Other works include a fine run of Hennepin, with his *Louisiana*, Paris, 1683, and Nuremburg, 1689; *Nouvelle Discoverie*, Utrecht, 1697 and 1698, and (rarest of all), *Nouveau Voyage*, Utrecht, 1698 and (in Spanish), Brussels, 1699.

Other classics deserving mention are a copy of Purchas's *Pilgrimage*, London, 1625-6, in original vellum; De Bry's *Voyages* with the *Elenchus*, 1617-1634, the beautiful Baron Landau copy; Cook's *Voyages*, all volumes including the folio atlas in original boards. This is a mere sampling from five hundred books in this field.

The main emphasis in Mr. Lilly's 18th-century Americana is naturally on the Revolution and Constitutional development, though many of the important milestones of American history are represented along with books continuing the history and exploration of Florida, Canada and the Mississippi Valley. Cotton Mather's *Magnalia Christi Americana*, London, 1702, is a large-paper copy with the two leaves of errata; there are fine Benjamin Franklins including the *Autobiography* in its first French, English, German and American editions. Of two copies of Thomas Jefferson's privately printed *Notes on Virginia*, Paris, 1782, one is inscribed, and the copy of the first census of the United States is signed by him. John Filson's *Kentucke*, Wilmington, 1784 (with the map), is among treasures which include the original broadside printing of the *Declaration of Independence*, together with its first appearance in a newspaper, a book, a magazine, and in England.

Hamilton's *The Federalist* is on thick paper; Franklin's printing of *Constitutions des Treize-Etats-Unis de l'Amerique* is on large paper and is George III's copy; and the official printing of the first *Acts of Congress* containing the *Bill of Rights* is the copy which Washington gave Jefferson--the first President to the first Secretary of State.

The expanding panorama of American life in the 19th century is reflected in such works as Lewis and Clark's *History*, in original printed boards; the first issue of the sheet music of *The Star Spangled Banner*; a beautiful set of the elephant folio Audubon and a mint set, in wrappers, of the popular issue in one hundred parts. The Civil War collection contains fine Lincoln material, including the *Second Inaugural*, one of only three known; a transcript of Daniel Emmett's *Dixie*; the proofs of the *Constitution of the Confederate States*, corrected by its vice-president, Alexander H. Stephens and believed unique; R. E. Lee's autograph surrender (General Order No. 9), and much related matter.

The collection of American literature runs into thousands of volumes. From the generally accepted 'first novel,' *The Power of Sympathy*, Boston, 1789, to Hemingway's *The Old Man and the Sea*, New York, 1952 (one of the first thirty special copies), almost all the important works in both verse and prose are present, many in presentation copies, with letters and manuscripts, and many of the author-collections are complete. The main interest before the Civil War is early fiction (about half the titles, and among these the rarest, in Oscar Wegelin's list of early American fiction, before 1825, are in the Library); southern fiction; the classic New England authors; and especially Edgar Allan Poe. After the Civil War there is a remarkable holding of Mark Twain, and a remarkable concentration of the famous Hoosier (Indiana) school of writers. Cooper's *The Spy* and Bryant's *Poems* (1821) were respectively the first American novel and the first American book of verse to receive international acclaim. Only one inscribed copy of each is known and both are in the Library.

Most of the substantial Poe collections are still privately owned and among those in public institutions only the New York Public Library's holdings can compete with Mr. Lilly's. No other university library has anything remotely comparable. It need only be said that the Lilly copies of all Poe's books are first editions. *Tales* (New York, 1845), in original wrappers, is a presentation copy of the correct first issue, and in this state the rarest of all Poe's works. There are numerous other presentation copies, manuscripts of *Eulalie* and *To Margaret*, his love letters to Sarah Helen Whitman, and their application for a marriage license. There is also a large collection of the magazines to which Poe contributed, including his own copy of Volume II of *The Broadway Journal* and much concerning the Poe circle.

Finally, it should be mentioned that Mr. Lilly's father founded the Foster Hall in Pittsburgh, with its Stephen Foster collection, and that his brother has been extremely active and generous in the Indiana Historical Society. And the Lilly Endowment, alone among such American foundations known to me, has been a generous and constant backer of antiquarian and bibliographical projects. Its recent *Twenty Year Report* reveals, for example, that $277,000 have been granted during the past fourteen years to the Bibliographical Society of America, mostly for the monumental Bibliography of American Literature; $40,000 to the Library of Congress towards the publication of the *Catalogue of the Library of Thomas Jefferson*; $30,000 to the American Antiquarian Society; and $20,000 to the New York Public Library.

In this 'Briefe and True Relation' of a single collector's achievement much has had to be left out. In the space available, only the great books could be mentioned and lesser works--some twenty thousand--have had to be passed over.

Mr. Lilly was fortunate in the period of his collecting, for the depression of the 1930s brought out treasures which would otherwise have never come his way, and substantially diminished competition. Happily, he never lost either his enthusiasm or his resources; and he was generally, as he deserved to be, well served by his advisers. No individual American collector to my knowledge has ever set out to do just what Mr. Lilly has done over so wide and varied a field. Morgan, Huntington, Folger and their like may have formed libraries worth more commercially, and certainly many American collectors have surpassed him in their specialized fields; but none has been so all-embracing.

5

J. K. LILLY –

AMERICA'S QUIET COLLECTOR (1966)

Josiah Kirby Lilly was a longtime customer and valued friend of Mr. Randall and was instrumental in bringing Randall to Indiana University to take charge of the library he established there. This heartfelt tribute was published shortly after Mr. Lilly's death in 1966. [From Antiquarian Bookman, *37 (June 27, 1966); 2679-2681.]*

THE late J.K. Lilly, of Indianapolis, Indiana was the most retiring, shy and unassuming collector of his generation, and also among its greatest.

He came to public notice when he presented his collection of some 20,000 first editions of English, American and Continental literature, manuscripts, Americana and books illustrating the history of science and thought to Indiana University in 1956. Valued then at $5,000,000, the *New York Times* reported it the single most important library of its kind ever given to an American educational institution. Which it was. The library housing it and bearing the family name was dedicated on October 3, 1960.

Though his first collecting love was books, and it is by his library that he is best known, this was only one of his amazingly varied collecting interests. As unobtrusively as he assembled his library he pursued his other avocations - always alone, always within a strict budget - selecting only individual pieces of highest quality and making his own decisions as to what to acquire. He had no librarian or curator - he was his own. He never bought bulk, seldom bid at auctions, and never purchased anything without having personally examined it.

So quietly was all this done that many collector and dealer

friends with whom he shared some common interests never even suspected his ardent pursuit of other hobbies. He never lent anything to exhibitions, not even books to the Grolier Club, of which he was a long-time member. He had, of the Club's *One Hundred Books Famous in English Literature*, 94, and of its companion volume, *One Hundred . . . Famous American Books*, 89. Only the few friends who visited what he was pleased to call his "play-house" which contained the collections had even an inkling of his vast interests, and even to them he seldom showed everything.

The first impression one got upon entering his private museum, which he designed himself, was of walls lined with toy soldiers, all immaculately housed in lighted glass cases - row after row of them, case after case, through one whole room and part of another.

This particular collection had begun with the European standards: from medieval knights on to Napoleon and his marshals, etc. But Lilly was never one to be confined by the conventional and traditional, or even, sometimes, by what was available. He decided, a few years ago, to buy a coupé. The first car he ever owned was a coupé, but he discovered that no one manufactured them anymore - and hadn't for years. Undismayed, he promptly commissioned Rolls-Royce to produce one, which they did. But to return to soldiers. Discovering that what Europeans had done to commemorate their past in this manner, Americans hadn't, he characteristically set about to remedy this.

He contracted for the exclusive services of a toy manufacturer for several years. They turned out a complete record in miniatures of every regiment which ever served in the United States Armies, with accurate uniforms, flags, insignia, arms, etc., up to 1900. The result is inspiring, to say the least. There are perhaps 5,000 soldiers: if one wants to see how New York's "Zouaves" were uniformed, or Pennsylvania's "Bucktails" or any other regiment, North or South, here they are. Included in the displays at suitable intervals are montages, the last and most spectacular being the entrance of the allied forces into Peking at the end of the rebellion, all done to scale and researched down to the Boxer's heads impaled over the gates.

The writer of these notes never knew, until years later, why Lilly suddenly developed an absorbing interest in American military costume books, not the easiest to come by, even 30 years ago. When I asked him later why he hadn't told me what he was up to in buying these books he replied, in effect: "You're a bookman and you got the necessary tools for me. My interest in toy soldiers would only have bored and possibly annoyed you." This seemed a key remark, to me. He never inflicted his passions and enthusiasms on anyone he thought would not be interested in them. He had many compartments which he kept locked.

Guns were another hobby - especially small arms, of which he had hundreds, an especial prize being an example of the first Colt revolver every manufactured - "the gun that won the West." I think there are only four in existence. And he had, of course, the equally rare second, differing, as I recall, in some loading and trigger guard details. But his pride was his Kentucky rifles - beginning with their first appearance in Pennsylvania and tracing their progress Westward, he had, he thought, an example of every type turned out by every manufacturer. And they were conditioned and in working order - he saw to that. He had loaded and fired most if not all of them.

He loved the sea and spent a great deal of his summer time at Falmouth, Mass. An ardent yachtsman, he somewhere along the line became interested in the history of the America's Cup series. In trying to discover pictures, details, etc., of the various American yachts which have held this trophy since its origin, he ran into difficulties, gaps, lack of precise information, etc. That was challenge enough. He had made a notable maritime collection and decided to add to it a complete set, done in exact miniature scale, of every American yacht winner. As they didn't exist, he had them made, all worked up from the original plans.

As a side-light on his love of the sea, it should be recorded that, rather late in life, he became interested in painting, and all his "scapes" are sea-scapes - frigates, schooners, harbors, waves, etc. All done with a passion for accuracy and, to my eye, a true feeling for the sea. "Though," he once confessed, "I can't get waves like Winslow Homer."

He asked me, many years ago, if I knew of any list of "100 Good Sea Novels." I answered "No, of course not, and if you want one you will have to make it yourself." A considerable while later I asked if he had decided on his list. His answer was: "No, not yet. I've only read 1,100 and I'm sure there are some good ones I've missed." Only recently he remarked: "You know, Childer's *The Riddle of the Sands* is getting close to the top." In the last year of his life he reread most of Stevenson and all of Conrad. When failing health caused him, a few years ago, to "swallow the anchor and return to the farm," as he said, this entire collection was given to the Marine Historical Association.

If should be remarked that when he commissioned work to be done for him, on toy soldiers, display cases, America's Cup Defenders, designing a private museum, or whatnot, he supervised every detail, and knew what he was about. He was an expert craftsman and delighted in doing his own cabinet work. "The secret of this," he once remarked, "is very simple. Measure twice and cut once." And when he finished with an enterprise he was completely finished. After he gave his library to Indiana University he ceased book collecting. He made a gracious appearance at the library's dedication and could never be enticed to return. He continued generous financial support and was always interested in its exhibitions and acquisitions, but he could not be persuaded to revisit. When he presented his collection to the University he was asked if there were any restrictions attached to the gift. His reply was: "No, I do not believe in the power of the dead hand. If you need a good football team, which you do, feel free to sell my Shakespeare to buy it if you wish."

But to return to his major collections, the record of these must be made by competent specialists. His stamps are among the finest, as a group, now in private hands in America. A recently publicized stamp sold well into five figures, and I happened to ask him if he had acquired it. "No," was the reply, "but when I saw that report, I thought I had it and looked it up, and I did. I bought it in the '30's. I thought it was under-rated then, and it was." He mentioned once that he started with American uncanceled revenue stamps and was "led on, the way you are, you know, into a world-wide field." "There are 100,000 stamps I want," he once told me (some years ago), "and I've only got 65,000 of them." (At his death, he had 77,000).

Gold coins are another collection. Viewing them is an experience. There is, I believe, only one lacking to complete his American set. But the coins he delighted to show were those of platinum, minted by the Russians in the 1830's. This collection (there are over 5,000 gold coins) takes high rank among those assembled anywhere at any time in the Western world.

Complementary to these is a small but choice collection of jewels: "My final folly," he recently exclaimed as he exhibited matched sets of stones - diamonds, rubies, emeralds and sapphires in small black cases, ranging each from one to ten carats.

I am not competent to speak of these glories, or of his eighteenth century paintings. There are only a few of these, a dozen or so. His last major purchase in this field was a Goya. He also had a small collection of portraits of historical and literary figures, among which is the last portrait of Lincoln. And when he could not find something to his liking, he had it created, an example being his commission to Boris Chaliapin to paint Theodore Dreiser.

It should be emphasized that while doing all this collecting he was leading a busy business life. The year before he left for France, in World War I, he entered the family pharmaceutical business, which was just beginning an era of great expansion. He then wrote a personnel policy for the company that is still regarded as a very model of its kind: "The greatest business problem today is the human problem of labor and the wise handling of employees," he stated, at the age of 23, fifty years ago.

He projected this view into his collecting. He made his errors and misjudgments; he was used (and misused) on occasion; deceits, fakes, forgeries and misplaced confidences caused heartaches and regrets. But he loved what he was doing and persisted in doing it despite betrayals. He was a fast student and he hit hard in whatever direction he spent his energies. When one famed dealer misrepresented something to him (through ignorance, not fraud), Lilly dropped him, later remarking, "I didn't intend to let him learn his business at my expense."

Intolerant of ignorance, his own or anyone else's, where information was not available, he sought it out. When his interests turned to books dealing with science and medicine and the bibliographical guides then available were not sufficient for his needs, he summoned W. R. LeFanu, Librarian of the Royal College of Surgeons, and I. Bernard Cohen, of Harvard, to his assistance. He always went to the top.

Among his vast philanthropies, the support of bibliographical projects was his favorite. He made many gifts, anonymous where possible, to the American Antiquarian Society, the Pierpont Morgan Library, the Library of Congress, the Bibliographical Society of America, the Indiana Historical Society, etc. It is due entirely to his zeal that bibliographies of Hoosiers Ade, Riley, Tarkington, and others, were done. He made a complete collection of a favorite childhood author, Harry Castlemon, and commissioned Jacob Blanck to do a bibliography. It was his interest that supported *American Heritage Magazine* in its early years. Yet when it was suggested that this magazine was the perfect medium for a series of articles on his collection of soldiers, he quietly said no.

In E. Millicent Sowerby's "Compiler's Preface" to the first volume of the magnificent *Catalogue of the Library of Thomas Jefferson,* issued by the Library of Congress, there is a line: "First of all, our appreciative thanks are due to Mr. Josiah K. Lilly, Jr., of Indianapolis, Indiana, through whose interested consideration this Project was supported." There are many such acknowledgements in other bibliographical works.

The work he was proudest of sponsoring was unquestionably the *Bibliography of American Literature* compiled by Jacob Blanck for the Bibliographical Society of America. The first volume of this monumental undertaking (Yale University Press, 1955), which is still continuing, is dedicated: "To the Directors of Lilly Endowment, Inc., of Indianapolis, and more particularly to the President of that organization, Josiah K. Lilly."

This work originated in 1943 and in large part was pushed into orbit by his faith and enthusiasm alone, against no inconsiderable amount of academic and other opposition which rather derided American literature and sought to divert the funds to what were considered more scholarly projects. He lived to see his judgment in this, and other decisions, richly vindicated.

I can speak from first-hand knowledge only of his library. Others have assembled more important collections of some of its segments, but taken as a unit it is by far the greatest, in any way you define that adjective, assembled by anyone in his era. There are, I have been told, individual collections of stamps, coins, paintings, and perhaps guns, which are individually superior to any of those assembled by him. And there are those who have spent upon such pursuits much more money. But there has been no one who even approached his combined achievement or who so completely realized his own vision of what he desired to accomplish. It should be mentioned incidentally, that through five vital years, 1941-1946, during which time he would normally have been at the height of his collecting career, he bought nothing. I can only speak for bookmen, but these years spanned the A. Edward Newton through the Frank Hogan sales, when an enormous amount of things of the type that interested him came on the market. I assume this happened in other fields. In any event, he bought nothing, on principle.

The public knowledge of any of a dozen of his avocations would have made him well-known had he cared for such fame. He simply didn't. His expressed philosophy was "You have done something worthwhile when you have taken something that is ugly and replaced it with something beautiful." He quietly accomplished a multitude of such transformations. And just as quietly he surrounded himself with the best he could find of the objects which expressed the ideas he loved. He was the *beau ideal* of the perfect collector.

6

TAMERLANE (1964)

*Mr. Lilly's Poe collection was one of his great achievements and it
was one of David Randall's favorites. As a Christmas keepsake
for 1964, Mr. Randall published a book to describe the formation
of the collection. The book opens with this discussion of the
great rarity, "Tamerlane."* [From *The J.K. Lilly Collection of Edgar
Allan Poe: An Account of Its Formation.* Bloomington: Indiana
University, The Lilly Library, 1964, pp. 1-10.]

J. K. Lilly's book collecting began about 1925 with an attempt to
gather complete collections of first editions of Indiana
authors--Tarkington, Ade, Dreiser, Wallace, Riley, *et al.* Most
works of these Hoosiers were then and are now readily available
and, with few exceptions, inexpensive. In 1927 Lilly became
enamored with the idea of forming a collection of Edgar Allan
Poe--an entirely different matter. Poe was, and is, the glamor boy
of the American collecting scene. The decision was an audacious
one, considering the youth and inexperience of the collector, the
times, and the competition to be faced. Yet in the short space of
about seven years he was able to bring together one of the finest
Poe collections ever assembled; indeed most of the major items
had been acquired by 1931. How this was done, with what care
and discrimination and mistakes, is recorded here.

The story is typical of Lilly's distinguished career as a
collector, a record of close personal attention to detail, the most
careful scrutiny of condition, with rigid rejection of inferior copies,
the seeking of expert advice and, sometimes, the disregarding of
it. He was patient and occasionally lucky. It should be

remembered that Poe was, at this time, only one of the many collecting interests, bookish and otherwise, to which Lilly devoted what time he could spare from a busy business career.

Of all the literature of American writers, the first editions, letters, manuscripts, and memorabilia of Poe are the most avidly sought and bring the highest prices. There are writers whose printed works are rarer (Thomas Holly Chivers is one) and whose autographs and manuscripts are harder to come by (Herman Melville, for example), but for collectors none has that peculiar attraction Poe possesses.

After his death, as in his life, controversy rages around Edgar Allan Poe. Usually neglected or abused in his own country during the decades following his death, he was adored in France, where he was translated by Baudelaire. When Rufus Griswold had silenced most American supporters with his vitriolic sketch, except Sarah Helen Whitman, he found others in England who quarreled among themselves, characteristic of Poe followers.

When the collecting of American literature began to be fashionable, in the last decades of the past century, Poe had already worked his magic, and from the very beginning he dominated the scene. There was a mystery, and still is, about the circumstances surrounding many of his publications which fascinates those interested in such things. This has resulted to the present day in dubious Poe attributions, forged manuscripts (the most successful, implausibly enough, by James Whitcomb Riley), thefts, prison sentences, suicide, and, on occasion, happy endings.

The circumstances of the publication of his first book, *Tamerlane and Other Poems*, Boston: Calvin F. S. Thomas . . . Printer, 1827--the so-called "black tulip" of American literature--remain obscure. Absolutely nothing is known about its printing, or its suppression, and next to nothing about its printer. Its very existence was unknown for many years, and Poe himself ignored his bantling. It is a small booklet of 40 pages, 6 7/8" x 5 5/16", bound in tan printed paper wrappers. Notices of its publication, but no reviews, are recorded.

It was a juvenile effort if there ever was one. The Preface reads: "The greater part of the Poems which compose this little volume, were written in the year 1821-2, when the author had not completed his fourteenth year. They were of course not intended for publication; why they are now published concerns no one but himself."

This is all we know about the book except for Poe's only other reference in his second volume, *Al Aaraaf, Tamerlane and Minor Poems*, Baltimore, 1829, which contains the note to *Tamerlane*: "Advertisement. This poem was printed for publication in Boston, in the year 1827, but suppressed through circumstances of a private nature."

As late as 1874 W. H. Ingram, writing on Poe's *Early Poems*, comments that the 1827 volume has "disappeared without a trace" and says of the 1829, "it does not appear possible now to obtain a copy." He uses for his *Early Poems* the New York, 1831 edition, with "Second Edition" on the title page, which was dedicated to "The U.S. Corps of Cadets," much to their amusement.

The first copy of *Tamerlane*, and for a long time the only one known, was sold by the famous dealer Henry Stevens of Vermont, who was acting as agent in purchasing American books for the British Museum. He bought it, he states in his *Recollections of James Lenox*, from "Mr. Samuel G. Drake as one of the poet's pieces, in Boston in 1859. It was sent into the Museum in 1860 with many other Boston tracts, and was paid for in 1867 for one shilling!" For many years it was considered unique. When acquired by the Museum it was in its original wrappers, but these were discarded when the book was rebound!

The best account of the discovery of other copies that I know is given by the late Charles E. Goodspeed in his *Yankee Bookseller* (Boston, 1937). The curious are referred to this excellent work. Briefly, the next copy was bought for fifteen cents by a Boston bookstore clerk, who sold it at auction in 1892 for $1,850. It passed through several owners into the hands of Frederic R. Halsey of New York.

The third copy to appear, at Richmond, Virginia, it is said, also wound up in Mr. Halsey's collection. He thus had two of the three known copies. Halsey sold most of his collection to Henry E. Huntington, retaining one of his *Tamerlanes*. This copy came up at auction in 1919 and brought $11,600. One other copy, "in sheets" (i.e., lacking wrappers), had been discovered in 1914 and bought by W. A. Clark of California, who issued a facsimile of it.

Thus, from 1827 to 1925 four copies of this work were on record. Then Vincent Starrett, "the great Cham" of booklovers, the

Elia of our time, wrote an article for the *Saturday Evening Post* entitled "Have You a Tamerlane in Your Attic?"

An old lady living in Worcester, Massachusetts, did. She dispatched a letter to Starrett, who was on vacation. Never in his wildest dreams had he imagined his article would turn up a copy. After fruitlessly awaiting a reply, she wrote to Charles Goodspeed. He, too, took his good time about considering her copy, but when he saw it, it was *IT*. A half hour after he had left the owner's home with the book, a letter from Starrett, eager for more details, arrived! This copy passed to Owen D. Young for $17,500 and is now in the New York Public Library. Here is Goodspeed's story of his second copy:

It was hardly a year after this that another Tamerlane was offered to me. The owners had read about my sale and came to tell me of the copy which they had bought at an auction sale of antiques some years before. Would they sell it? That depended. What was it worth?

It so happened that at the moment I had a good customer who wanted a Tamerlane and was willing to pay more for it than Mr. Young gave me for Mrs. Dodd's copy. I put my cards on the table. I told my callers what was not then generally known--the amount which the other copy had brought and offered them that sum. They decided they would wait. "It isn't growing any less valuable," one remarked. "That is true," I replied, "assuming that no more copies turn up soon, but if they do the value of yours might suffer." "We will chance that," he replied, as they took leave.

Here the matter rested for the time, but later I made another attempt to do business with these people. I made an appointment with them, and my son, who was by that time handling the rare-book section of our business, went with me. After examining the book and finding it in fine condition, I said: "Mr. --- we have been dickering over this book for a year now and have got nowhere. Either you want to sell it or you don't. If you do, we will try to do business; if you don't, we will drop the matter." "What is your offer?" he asked. In reply, I took from my pocket a check for eighteen thousand dollars, handed it to him, saying as I did so, "Here is my offer." He took the check, looked it over, and handed it back with a cool "That's a good *offer!*"

It looked like a stalemate. I tore up the check and started to leave the room, saying that if he did not wish to sell the book it was useless to waste time in talking further about it. "Oh! I will sell," was his reply. "How can you sell it if you don't put a price on it?" I asked. "But I have a price."

"What is it?" "I'll sell it for twenty thousand dollars." At last we had a definite figure. It was a stiff one, but my customer, an Indiana collector, wanted the book, and I paid the amount. This buyer has two other Poe first editions which came from us, the Tales and The Raven in Wiley and Putnam's Popular Library, 1845--not great rarities ordinarily, but these copies are in unused condition, the paper covers bright and fresh as when they left the binders. It is doubtful if such another pair exists.

This was Mr. Lilly's first major purchase of a rare book. As he once remarked to me, "There is nothing like beginning at the top and working down." Lilly had requested that no publicity be given his purchase, but somehow his name got out and reams of unwanted newspaper stories followed. He was, of course, swamped with offers of old books and antiques, none of the slightest value, and eventually had to draw up a form letter for reply. One of the most amusing communications he received was a penciled note on yellow paper, printed in block letters:

If you will put ten thousand dollars ($10,000) under the big white stone under the west end of the Eagle Creek Bridge just east of the Insane Asylum at midnight Nov. 18th just one night later at same time and place you will find the original copy of the Ten Commandments [sic].

Of more annoyance was a claim that the book had been stolen. On April 16, 1929, Lilly wired Goodspeed:

Have been approached by accredited detective agency as to source my copy Tamerlane Stop Statement made same copy stolen summer of nineteen twenty-eight Stop Please advise name of Nashua man from whom you procured book and other pertinent data Stop Feel we should render every assistance in tracing theft Stop Immediate reply suggested.

Mr. Goodspeed called Lilly and wrote him the same day:

Confirming our telephone conversation of today. The people who have been bothering you represent, they say, a man named Finney (possibly it is Phinney) a marble or monumental manufacturer in Philadelphia. Their story in brief is something like this.
This man's father (who died recently) about three years or more ago had a copy of Tamerlane which he loaned with two other books to a man

whose name I do not now recall. This man was a stone-mason and I assume might have been an employee of Mr. Finney's. This man took these three books up to New York state where he had a farm-house. Later he closed the house and went to the western part of the state. While absent his house was burglarized and he discovered that the Tamerlane was missing. He reported the loss of it to the Captain of the State Constabulary who perhaps a couple of months or so ago wrote us on account of this man's having seen in the newspapers that we had sold a copy of the book. Just why he took no steps of this kind until this winter when his loss occurred last summer does not transpire. The Pinkerton Assistant Superintendent, who called upon me, stated that in their client's copy of the book the name of Finney was written. We explained to him that the copy of the book we had had no name in it and had to our knowledge been in the possession of the individual from whom we bought it, from 1927 to the time we bought it in 1928. Inasmuch as the book which Mr. Finney had would appear to have been in his possession, or in the possession of the man to whom he loaned it since 1926 at least and that the family name of Finney was written in it on the first page, it would seem from his own statement that it could have no connection with the copy which we sold you.

If these facts did not exist there could still be no question as to the book being the property of the man from whom we dealt as this party is a man of high standing in the community and could have had no possible connection with any illegal transaction resulting from the burglary.

Mr. Jones, the Assistant Superintendent of the Pinkerton Agency in this city with whom I have talked, says that he will write to the Philadelphia office today asking them to inform the Indianapolis Agency of this fact so that they will not be of any further annoyance to you.

The whole thing is preposterous and the representations made concerning its existence and loss seem highly improbable.

This apparently ended that matter.

It should be noted that Goodspeed speaks of the *Tales* and *The Raven* he had sold the "Indiana collector . . . . It is doubtful if such another pair exists." Indeed it is. They are in literally new condition and were sold to Lilly in 1934 for $1,000. On receiving them he wrote:

Of course I will retain the two Poe books sent forward with the distinct understanding that you will write me a letter and tell me where in the world these turned up and what your speculations are as to how and why the condition of said books is "as is" after lo, these many years. Have you ever seen such fine copies of these two titles before? I can't help wondering if you have found a stack of these books about eight or ten feet high, packed away in cotton.

To which George Goodspeed replied:

I don't wonder that you are curious as to the source of the Poe books. They were a part of the library of the late Fred Holland Day of Norwood, Massachusetts. Mr. Day was a member of the publishing firm of Copeland & Day, which had a brief and aesthetically successful career in Boston during the middle 90's. The venture was an unprofitable one, and was not continued after 1898.

They were the publishers of Stephen Crane's "The Black Riders," of "Songs from Vagabondia," and of many of Louise Imogen Guiney's and Alice Brown's books of that period.

Mr. Day, who for the last twenty years of his life was a recluse, was always a book collector, and in his earlier days showed a good deal of interest in Poe, but curiously enough these two books were the only first editions of Poe that he had. It is my impression that he bought them in New York, probably about forty years ago.

I have never seen a copy of either book in comparable condition, and there surely is no stack of them about so far as I am aware.

The wide publicity attendant on every *Tamerlane* transaction has since flushed out other copies--fourteen are now recorded, not all perfect. This has tended (as Goodspeed predicted) to depress prices to the point where the book, though still a five-figure item, has only once exceeded the price Lilly paid for it. The last auction record, the Bemis-Frank J. Hogan copy, 1945, was $15,500; several copies have changed hands since at a lower figure.

On the other hand, there was in the very Goodspeed, 1925, catalogue from which Owen D. Young purchased the *Tamerlane* a fine set of the Audubon folio edition of his *Birds of America* priced at $3,500. Mr. Lilly had the opportunity to acquire this but waited until he purchased one from Scribner's, in 1939, for $15,000. Today a set comparable to Goodspeed's or Lilly's would bring more than $50,000. The whirly-gig of taste is, in the rare book field, a chancy thing and "buying for investment" unwise. If one wants to gamble, there are always Wall Street and fifty-two cards in a deck.

7

BOOK COLLECTING AS A HOBBY (1953)

This advice to beginning book collectors was broadcast over radio station WNYC in New York City as part of a week long Festival of Books. [From Antiquarian Bookman, 11 (April 11, 1953): 1283-1285.]

Many people accumulate books, few people build a library. This is the difference, it seems to me, between book-buying and book-collecting. All people who collect books are book-buyers, but few book-buyers are book-collectors. Aside from buying books there is only one other way I know of acquiring them, and that this breaks down into two departments: stealing them or, which too often amounts to the same thing, borrowing them. Neither method is likely to result in a truly satisfactory library. In the first case one is liable to be caught and either fined or imprisoned or both, and in the second case one's friends may be inconsiderate enough not to have available for borrowing the books one really wants.

Purchase, therefore, remains the best method so far devised of acquiring a library. Now, however casual your bookbuying may have been in the past, it is certain that you have bought what you liked to read, or thought you might sometime like to read, or (perhaps too often) what some reviewer persuaded you you ought someday to say you have read. This has resulted in a collection of volumes, but not in a library, and though you are buying books you are not collecting them. Nor are you having the fun and the excitement of creating a unit distinctly your own.

I cannot emphasize too strongly that the formation of a library, or the collecting of books as a hobby, is not exclusively, or even primarily, a hobby for rich and leisured people only. It is a game where knowledge counts as much as money and one can pursue it without involving oneself in bankruptcy, because anyone who can afford an occasional purchase of a new book can afford the occasional purchase of an old book and by collecting along a *plan* of what one likes, or whom one likes, over a short period one will have a distinctive library and not merely a lot of books.

There are benefits which money cannot buy, but Gutenberg Bibles, first editions of Shakespeare and manuscripts of Charlotte Bronte are not among them. But one does not have to aim that high. Useful, enjoyable and valuable collections have been and still are being assembled for very modest outlays of cash indeed, though at considerable expense of time and research and with a lot of pleasure and fun and perhaps eventual profit thrown in.

I do not wish to foster an illusion that having formed a library about an author or a subject, you will be able to turn around and sell it at a large--or even a modest-- profit. You may be able to do so, but don't start with that premise and don't let anyone sell you the idea that book-collecting is a get-rich-easy scheme. I assure you it isn't. The value of any given book, old or new, five years from now, can be predicted by no one. Too many things can happen in that time to admit such prophecy.

But the *pleasure* you get from ownership, from reading, from sheer accumulation, the filling in of a gap here, and a lacking title there, will reward you more than you expect, and the cash value may be added for good measure.

Not all books are rare, neither are all rare books old. Nor, oddly enough are all rare books valuable. All depends upon the immutable law of supply and demand. If there is a book, say two hundred years old, of which only one copy is recorded, this does not mean that it is of great, or even of any value, if no one wants it. It may be perhaps a theological treatise of a long-winded nature, published by its author to satisfy his vanity by seeing his name in print. No one cared then and no one cares now, whether it was printed or not, except its author and he is no longer available to purchase it.

On the other hand, the first book of poetry by a now successful contemporary author may literally be worth its weight in gold. Elinor Wylie's *Incidental Numbers* (1912) is an example. Or Einstein's first brief formula of his famous theory (1905) is another. Or the first printing of the *Communist Manifesto* is a third. None of these is easily come by, they are *wanted* by more people than can easily acquire copies, and therefore sell at a premium over their published price--in these cases a very considerable premium. Now, of the first mentioned work, *Incidental Numbers*, the prospective owner must perforce buy a first edition for the simple reason that there is no other. The book was never reprinted nor will it ever be. Of the other books mentioned, he can, if he is interested in them, buy their texts for twenty-five cents in any store. Such an edition may satisfy the student but it will not satisfy the collector who wants his books, whenever possible, to be a first edition or one distinguished by perhaps its beauty of typography or binding or illustration, qualities not possessed by a twenty-five cent reprint.

This may be, indeed is, a selfish and sensual feeling but one which among collectors is universal. It is a feeling one either has, or doesn't have, and that holds true of collecting postage stamps, campaign buttons, meerschaum pipes, or anything else an individual fancies.

And let me add here, by the way, that book-collectors do use and read what they collect. The cartoonists who delight in picturing the wretched plight of the man surrounded by thousands of books who has nothing he can read is a victim of his own imagination. The non-reading book-collector was first held up to scorn, in English at least, in 1509 when Richard Pynson of London issued *The Ship of Fools*, Alexander Barclay's translation of Sebastian Brandt's *Das Narrenschiff* which had been published at Basel in 1494.

But it is simply not true, never was and--until book-buyers and book-borrowers in general begin to read in as heavy a proportion as book-collectors--it will never be.

I have sold both old and new books for a fair number of years and in my experience there is more hokum in run-of-the-shop bookbuying and book-borrowing and books-of-the-moment lending than there ever has been in book-collecting.

What makes the usual sex-spiced bestseller? Intrinsic merit? A reputation based on solid past achievement by the author? An honest appreciation of artistic sincerity? Devotion to a durable novelty in style or treatment? None of these. The supreme inspiration, alas, is the age-old incentive to keep up with Literate Lizzie.

The collector, on the other hand, acquires his books from his personal conviction of their value and interest to him, and knows a very considerable amount indeed about what's inside their covers.

To most people, the first editions of works of literature are so strongly accented in contemporary collecting that they are likely to regard that as the whole story. Actually it is far from being so. Very often a later edition is of much more interest and value than the original--perhaps because the author has made significant changes or additions.

Thomas Campbell's *The Pleasures of Hope* was first published in 1799 and was highly regarded indeed by our forefathers, but today we ignore it and we search for the much later seventh edition because it is in that his famous poems appear, including *Hohenlinden* and *Lochiel's Warning* with its often-quoted lines: "Tis the sunset of life gives me mystical love, And coming events cast their shadows before." And it is the third edition of Harry Carey's *Poems* which first contains the immortal *The Ballad of Sally in Our Alley*. Or in science, for example, it is in the second edition of Robert Boyle's *New Experiments* (1662), that we find his famous table indicating the reciprocal relation between pressure and the volume of a gas--the first statement of Boyle's law--and, while we are on this subject, one has to acquire a third edition (1807) of Thomas Thomson's *A System of Chemistry* to read, in its first appearances in print, John Dalton's epoch-making atomic theory in its application to the density of the atoms of gases.

As we have indicated, the non-collector is likely to feel that only the original editions of books of literary or historical significance are of value or are collected. This is not so. To the person with a specific hobby any book of importance in his field is desirable. He may want books on bee-keeping, cooking, navigation, fishing, smoking--whatever anyone's trade or profession or even pet aversion, it can be paralleled in book-collecting. But in all of these categories, there have been thousands of books printed and hundreds now in print, and unless he wants (and can afford) to build a special library to house his accumulation--and some people have--he will have to exercise some discrimination as to what he purchases--choosing this edition for its text, another, perhaps, for its historical importance, another because he happens to like its type or binding and--ergo, he is on his way to becoming a collector because he must use selectivity of some kind. Usually he will find a guide of some sort--either in a bibliography devoted to his subject, or in a history of it, or whatnot.

Now, having decided to become a collector, or at any rate having decided upon some subject or author he would like to explore, how does he go about it? Well, if he happens to live in or near a reasonably large city, he can visit the local second-hand dealer, or all of them if the city is large enough to permit of their existence. Most (though not all) dealers are amiable and knowing persons and only too willing to help a beginning collector. If he does not keep anything in stock, the dealer will take the prospective customer's name and report when--and if--anything promising happens his way. Or he may offer to advertise in trade magazines dealing with old books and report what is quoted to him. Or our prospective collector can go to his local library and get from them the names and addresses of out-of-town dealers who may specialize in the type of material he is interested in.

A few letters sent off will bring in anything from a mimeographed list to a neatly printed and bound booklet which make, severally and collectively, the most fascinating reading in the world. The catalogues may come from auction houses and if there is something he wants he must make up his mind to bid immediately--those are now or never propositions--or at least be resigned to waiting perhaps a long time until the desired item turns up again. But if the catalogues come from dealers, they are usually willing to send the book along for inspection. At any rate, our collector is off--and good hunting to him.

But unless a person feels a definite urge to collect books as books--and gets fun out of doing so, he had better collect something else. There are many less wieldy things to gamble with, and will be while Wall Street endures and fifty-two cards constitute a deck.

8
KIPLING AND COLLECTING (1936)

When Mr. Randall wrote this essay, Rudyard Kipling was avidly collected. He is out of favor today, but Randall's comments on collecting contemporary authors are still instructive. [From *Publisher's Weekly*, 129 (January 25, 1936): 379-380.]

RUDYARD KIPLING was the earliest writer whose first editions were systematically and enthusiastically collected by his contemporaries. Their activities set the fashion for the collecting of moderns, and no writer in all book collecting history has ever had, during his lifetime, such devoted followers as his have proved themselves to be. Practically all the problems inherent in the collecting of "moderns" were first faced by Kipling collectors and their researches guided later enthusiasts when they in turn pursued other game.

The proof of these statements, if proof be needed, can be seen from even a casual examination of the procession of Kipling bibliographies, and of book auction records. Take the turn of the century for example. In the auction records of 1899, Barrie, Wilde and Hardy (the "Lord of the Wessex Coast"), were great figures, but collectors pretty generally ignored them. Their "firsts" appeared infrequently and brought an occasional few pounds, but Kipling is a different story. Practically all of his titles made regular appearances in the rooms, and in 1899, there are no fewer than 96 entries listed. The prices range as high as £26, a not inconsiderable price, though it was, to be sure, for a copy of "The Smith Administration," perhaps the same copy which on November 25, 1927, brought $14,000 at the Anderson Galleries, the all time high for a printed book by a living author. In short,

Kipling has been more collected, and at higher prices, than any other contemporary writer.

Partly this was because of his universal appeal, shown best perhaps in the enormous sales of his works. But largely, it has been because he was, and is, pre-eminently a "collector's author." Every pitfall of collecting and every joy, can be found in him. The difficulties of forming anything approaching a representative Kipling collection have been, from the very start of his career, formidable, but the difficulty of the chase has never yet deterred the pursuer.

A "complete Kipling collection" has never been formed, and never can be formed, for there are simply not enough copies of his rarities to go around. There have been notable collections, like McCutcheon's, and there are notable collections, like Ballard's, among others, but never a "complete" one.

Among the problems the Kipling collector has to face are those of rarity. The first issues of the "Indian Railway Library" can be obtained by an expenditure of cash, as can an "Echoes" and "Quartette," but where secure a first edition of "The City of Dreadful Night" (the Wheeler & Co. issue, suppressed, three copies only preserved, of which only one is known today)? "Departmental Ditties" can be picked up occasionally without the flap, and less occasionally with the flap, but try to obtain a fine copy with the flap *and* with the pink tape which bound it!

But rarities like these, rare because of the place of publication, or because of suppression, are but part of the Kipling collector's difficulties. There is the vexed, and still only partly solved problem of piracies, linking inevitably with the "follow the flag" controversy. If the collector wants the first appearance in book form of "Mandalay," "Danny Deever," or "Gunga Din," he must obtain, not the first book in which Kipling's audience read them ("Barrack Room Ballads and Other Verses," 1892), but he must have "Departmental Ditties, Barrack Room Ballads, and Other Verses," New York, 1890, and the correct issue of it at that. The manifold problems of the Kipling piracies are still far from solved, and even though bibliographical research has been long and lovingly pursued by such experts as E. V. Martindale, Lloyd H. Chandler, Flora Livingston, and others, discoveries of moment are still to be made. And the piracies gain added interest from the vitriolic battle Kipling waged against them.

Rarity in another form than by suppression or publication in India confronts the Kiplingite, centering around the copyright pamphlets, an offspring of his battles with the pirates. Where can one obtain the Doubleday, Page copyrights of, for example, "South America," or "The White Man's Burden" (the majority of even the copyright issue of which was destroyed by Kipling's orders), as well as other commoner titles?

There are, too, the newspapers and magazines--Kipling himself could not remember, or definitely identify, some of his early contributions, and it is not unlikely that hitherto unidentified material is still to be uncovered. And there is always the chance of the collector with a knowledge of Kipling and a nose for books coming across something startling. Witness the fairly recent unearthing of a copy or so of the first appearance of "The Female of the Species," in its first form (with the portrait of Kipling holding a cigarette, not a cigar), which was hitherto completely unknown. The collector of modest means, who knows his Kipling, has always had, and still has, because of the complexity of his bibliography, the opportunity for such a coup, so while he may not own a copy of "The Smith Administration," neither may its owner possess his especial "find."

It is this element which has intrigued so many collectors of Kipling, and will, in all probability, continue to do so. In addition, there are spurious, or falsely dated Kiplings, vide "In Sight of Mount Monadnock," privately printed in 1904, and again (still dated 1904), circa 1918. These problems of suppression, copyright, forgeries, unidentified contributions and so on, first faced the Kipling dealer and collector, and later the collector of modern firsts in general. They can say, and may it not be the least of Kipling's glories, that "they learned about collecting through him."

9
WAVERLY IN AMERICA (1935)

This discussion of the American editions of Sir Walter Scott's novels is an early example of Mr. Randall's long-standing interest in American editions of foreign works and foreign editions of American works. The essay elicited an appreciative letter from the noted English bibliographer R. W. Chapman whose book on cancels Randall had made use of in the essay. [From *The Colophon, A Quarterly for Bookmen*, New Series, 1 (Summer, 1935): 39-55.]

I *have heard from my father--a pioneer of Kentucky--that in the early days of this century men would saddle their horses and ride from all the neighboring counties to the principal posttown of the region when a new novel by the Author of Waverley was expected.* Speech of John Hay at the unveiling of the bust of Sir Walter Scott in Westminster Abbey, May 21, 1897.

The novels of Sir Walter Scott were America's first sensational bestsellers. It is not now generally realized just how avidly our fathers read and re-read his works, or how vast his influence was. William Edward Dodd says: "Few men ever had greater influence over the cotton planters than the beloved Scottish bard and novelist." Influence indeed! One is used to hearing Harriet Beecher Stowe blamed for helping foment the Civil War with *Uncle Tom's Cabin*, but the same charge has been brought against Scott, and by no other than Mark Twain: "Sir Walter Scott had so large a hand in making Southern character as it existed before the war, that he is in great measure responsible for the war."

It is probable that, though Scott's American popularity was not confined to the South, it waxed strongest there. *The Richmond Enquirer* of November 20, 1832, edged its columns with black on receiving news of his death, and it has been asserted that the original Ku Klux Klan owed its origin in part to the influence of *Anne of Geierstein.*[1] His influence was felt over the whole nation, and so large were the sales of his novels that entire editions of a new work would be sold out on the day of publication, and their printing and distribution became a hectic, cut-throat game, with booksellers and publishers striving for every advantage. Thus it came about that America, though it probably did not have the honor of reading his novels before any other nation, did have the opportunity of reading them more nearly as the author originally wrote them than did even his most ardent Scottish and English admirers. And thereby hangs our tale.

Following the startling success of *Waverley*, succeeding Scott novels were reprinted in America as soon after receipt of British copies as possible. But with every increasing success--almost every new novel outsold its precursor--competition became keener. J. and J. Harper and C. S. Van Winkle of New York, Lilly of Boston, Mathew Carey of Philadelphia, and numerous other houses battled for the books, and it became apparent that even a few days' advantage by any one of them over his competitors would enable the enterprising publisher to reap a small, if not well-merited, fortune on each publication.

Mathew Carey in particular saw his chance and, not being a man to hesitate, took it. Carey, a Dubliner born, had fled from Ireland to Paris, pursued by a vengeful government that charged him with publishing seditious literature, and while in Paris he met and admired Franklin and LaFayette. He returned, unwisely, to Dublin, and soon found himself in prison, with ample time to think about Franklin's land of the free. At any rate, he appeared in 1785 in Philadelphia with four hundred dollars, lent him by LaFayette, and immediately embarked on a vigorous and distinguished publishing career.

Carey saw the advantage to be gained by being the first to put Scott's new novels on the market and set out to devise some scheme for doing so. The question, obviously, was how to get copy ahead of his competitors. For if he could get it first, and have his books on the market before his rivals even began to set type, he would have perhaps a week's advantage--they would print immediately, of course, from his edition without waiting for exemplars of the British edition to arrive. But with a hungry South and a scarcely less eager North ready to buy from the first to offer, a week's start would be enough. It would not do to wait, as he and others had been waiting, for finished copies of the novels to arrive from abroad for that was already causing stalemate. Carey could possibly have dealt with Scott directly, but Scott was receiving such enormous sums for his work that his rates would probably have been prohibitive, and besides, pay money for what could be had without it? The Carey plan was to secure advance sheets, or, better yet, galley proofs, and set the type from these. Carey, with his transatlantic experience and friendships, could get them, and did get them, much to the annoyance of Scott's publisher, Archibald Constable, as witness the following letter:[2]

25 April, 1822

Wm Kerr Esq
GPO Edinb[urgh]

> *Having reason to believe that one or more of the workmen in Mr. Ballantyne's Printing Office are in the Practice of Abstracting sheets of works in the progress of Printing--more especially those of the Author of* Waverley, *and forwarding said Sheets by means of the Post Office to America, more particularly to Philadelphia, we beg to know if it is consistent with the rules of the Post Office to stop any such Sheets so transmitted in order to effect the detection of the person found abstracting our property in this manner.*

It is obvious from this letter that Carey succeeded in planting a workman in Ballantyne's printing office, or more probably in bribing a workman already there, to send him galleys of the novels, or sheets, as they came off the presses. Indeed, he may have had a secret agreement with Ballantyne for the purchase of sheets, for Ballantyne was exceedingly machiavellian, and though Scott had implicit faith in him, others, as Constable and Blackwood, seem just as thoroughly to have mistrusted him. However that may be, someone, apparently about 1822, began to send advance sheets or galleys to Carey, and continued to do so until the last of Scott's works were published.

Carey worked fiendishly when he received them.[3] Edward

Bradley says that the copy, when received, was apportioned to every printing house in Philadelphia, and the complete novel put in type in three days. "It was necessary to keep relays of compositors working over the early sheets night and day. When the binder had finished his works a stage coach had been chartered and a young employee, William A. Blanchard, later to become a partner, would gallop off to New York with the supplies. Mounted gallantly on a huge pile of *Waverley*, he would ride night and day, ferrying his precious cargo of romance across the North River to the waiting booksellers."

All this may be, perhaps, interesting as the first example of American literary piracy on a large scale--the phenomenon was to be duplicated again and again until the present imperfect copyright law was enacted. But it has an important bibliographical phase. Scott was a meticulous workman, forever revising, correcting and polishing his novels until the moment of publication and, ardent antiquarian that he was, intolerant of even the slightest error. Most of his manuscripts and proof-sheets have disappeared, but we have tangible and tantalizing proof of the extent of his revisions by the presence in his English first editions of numerous canceled leaves. Of the twenty-three titles of his *Waverley Novels*, twelve have cancelled leaves in first edition.

A cancelled leaf is proof positive of some last-minute textual change. There are, of course, other means of correcting errors-errata lists, primarily, but they disclose what was to be corrected and why. A cancel, on the other hand, is a challenge. It shows that a change has been made without giving any hint as to what the change was or the reason for it, and the conscientious editor, literary student, or admirer of the author's work, who would not have even a single word unrecorded, is faced, generally, with an insoluble puzzle unless a copy of the work turns up with the original leaf intended to be excised and replaced still intact--and it rarely does. (Following Mr. Chapman's[4] nomenclature this leaf will henceforth be called the *cancellandum*, and the new or corrected leaf which replaces it the *cancellan*.)

If the original leaf is not found, all sorts of vain imaginings arise to plague one's waking moments. The knowledge that a leaf has been cancelled, instead of being superfluous knowledge, becomes dangerous knowledge. If, when found, the reason for the cancellation proves to be trifling, at least its discovery has removed a source of irritation. And just what is 'trifling'? That is a problem for literary critic, historian and biographer; as Mr. Chapman puts it, "It is not for the bibliographer to decide what is of value to his betters; his business is to record the facts."

We have, then, the facts that Mathew Carey, Philadelphia printer, late of Dublin and Paris, through chicanery or otherwise secured advance sheets of Sir Walter Scott's *Waverley Novels* from the shop of Ballantyne, the Edinburgh printer; that he generally secured uncorrected sheets; that, therefore, textual examination of these sheets, reading against the cancellans in the British first editions, will show the changes made. Such are the facts. As to their interpretation, why, following Mr. Chapman's advice, I leave that to my betters.

The problem is simple, as none of the questions of the modus operandi of cancels need be faced. There is no need to untangle the problems of re-setting of type, the ordinary (and extraordinary) ways of placing a cancellans, the question of conjugate leaves, and so on. Indeed, one does not even have to detect the cancels, for that has been done by Greville Worthington. The question is purely one of textual comparison. Knowing of the existence of the cancellans, one need only compare the British text with the American text to reconstruct the cancellandum.

For example, pages 65-66 of Volume II of the English edition of the first series of *Chronicles of The Canongate* (1827) is a cancellans in all known copies. The corresponding passages occur on page 46 of Volume II of the American edition, and reading the texts against each other reveals the original error. Zilia Moncada is explicitly characterized in one sentence as "understanding no English," yet a few paragraphs later one character asks another a question in English which she overhears and understands. The original sentence, as Scott wrote it, and as it appears in the American edition, is: Zilia de Moncada heard the question; and it seemed as if . . . etc. Reading the sheets, however, Scott caught the inconsistency, and corrected the sentence to read in the English edition: Zilia de Moncado heard the question (which, being addressed to the father, Grey had inconsiderately uttered in French), and it seemed as if...etc. To make the correction at the late stage in which Scott discovered the inconsistency it was necessary to cancel the page, and this was done.

Mr. Van Antwerp attempted (and with marked success) to reconstruct the original text of the cancellandum by comparison with the original manuscript, where the manuscript was in existence and available. He realized, however, that "tracing cancels from manuscript alone is not the dependable method, because the really important clues are often found only in the uncancelled leaves or in the proofs." This is perfectly true, for it is only when an error is not caught until the final stages of printing that such expensive and drastic surgery as cancellation is resorted to. It should be remembered, by the way, that probably not all the errors listed below are Scott's, for so great was his desire for anonymity that neither his original manuscript nor corrected proof-sheets ever reached the printer--George Huntly Gordon, his secretary, or James Ballantyne copied everything he wrote. This practise continued until the failure of Constable, when the publication of their transactions forced Scott to public acknowledgment of his writings. Some of the errors listed below which necessitated last minute changes, therefore, may have been the copyists' errors and not Scott's.

There follows a list of the American editions of Scott's works published by the various Carey firms in which the British editions of the same titles have cancel leaves; a line-off of the American title-page; and, in parallel columns, enough of the text of the English cancellans and the corresponding American text, printed from the cancellandum, to explain the reason for the changes. All these American editions were issued in printed boards, uncut, or in boards with paper label, and are today of genuine rarity in original state.

THE PIRATE: /A Romance. /[rule] /By the Author of Waverley, Ivanhoe, &c. /[rule] /In Two Volumes. /Vol. I. [II.] /[double-rule] /Philadelphia: M. Carey & Sons, Chestnut Street. / 1822.

Worthington says: "Pages 17 and 18 (B 1) of Vol. II are cancelled in some copies. The original state of this leaf has the reading *their* as the last word of line 20; the second state has the reading *there*." The American edition has the reading *there*, which Worthington calls the second state, but I believe this to be the American printer's correction, since the error was an obvious one. The real cause of cancellation, however, was this:

English First Edition	American as above
Vol. II, last three lines of page 16 and first two lines of page 17.	Vol. I, page 197, lines 25-29,
He darted a deprecatory glance at Mordaunt, as if for the purpose of imploring secrecy respecting his tumble; and the Udaller, who saw his advantage, although he was not aware of the cause, etc., etc.	*He darted a glance at Mordaunt, as if for the purpose of imploring secrecy. The Udaller, who saw his advantage, although he was not aware of the cause, etc., etc.*

This change (giving the reason for "imploring secrecy") and the consequent re-wording is the real reason for the cancellation. Did the original leaf, the cancellandum, have the reading as given in the American edition, or was Carey here working from uncorrected page proof or galley proof? If the former, then pages 17 and 18 of the English edition, whether they have the reading *their* or *there*, are both cancellans, and one is not, as Worthington states, a cancellandum, the other a cancellans. This question can only be resolved by an examination of a copy of the English edition in original state with the reading *their*, to which I have not had access. All cancels are not, as Chapman points out, mounted on stubs, and their detection is sometimes difficult. It would be an interesting problem to solve, however, as it would prove whether, in this case at least, Carey's Ballantyne connection sent him galley-proofs.

PEVERIL OF THE PEAK. /By the Author of/"Waverley," "Kenilworth," &c. /"If my readers should at any time remark that I am par-/ ticularly dull, they may be assured there is a design under /it."--British Essayist. / [rule] /In Three Volumes. /Vol. I [II.III.] / [double-rule] / Philadelphia: /H. C. Carey and I. Lea--Chestnut Street. /And H. C. Carey & Co. No. 157, Broadway, New York. /[row of twelve dots] /1823.

Worthington says: "The following leaves are cancels: Vol. II, pp. 305-306 (U 1); Vol. III, pp. 15-16 (A 8); Vol. IV, pp. 253-254 (Q 7)."

English First Edition	American, as above
Vol. II, page 306, line 7. *Yesterday.*	Vol. II, page 102, line 6. *Today.* The error *Today* also appears in the author's original MS.
Vol. III, page 16, lines 1-2. *Seated themselves.*	Vol. II, page 117, line 28. *Kneeled down.* The reading *kneeled down* also appears in the author's original MS. Mr. Van Antwerp gives other differences between the MS and English cancellans; as the errors he lists in MS do not appear in the American edition, they were doubtless corrected in galley or page proof.
Vol. IV, page 253, line 4. *Betwixt his Grace and Chaffinch.*	Vol. III, page 157, line 4. *Betwixt them.* This reading also appears in the only known copy of the English edition containing the original cancellandum.

Working as they did, from sheets sent over at various times, the firm of Carey occasionally labored under difficulties, an example of which occurs in the present tale. The title-pages of Volumes I and II of the American edition are cancellans, and Volume III contains only about half as many pages as the other two volumes, thus giving the set a rather lopsided appearance. Examination of a copy in boards clearly reveals what happened. The American publishers invariably condensed the English three-deckers into two volumes. When the sheets for *Peveril of the Peak* began to arrive, they planned it as a two volume novel. The story turned out to be a long one (something Carey could not know in advance) and the English edition was printed in four volumes.

After setting up Volumes I and II, it was necessary for Carey to add a third volume; therefore the title-pages of Volumes I and II, which read "In Two Volumes," had to be cancelled, and new ones, reading "In Three Volumes," substituted.

I have never seen a copy of the American edition with the uncancelled title-pages to the first two volumes, but the above reasoning must account for the presence of the cancellans. This is borne out by the examination of the printed boards. Volumes II and III bear the note on the printed boards "In Three Volumes"; Volume I also bears this note, but it is on a slip pasted over the note originally printed, which was "In Two Volumes." This was verified by soaking off the slip with the note "In Three Volumes." Thus the title-pages of Volumes I and II and the printed boards of Volume I of the American edition had been printed before the discovery that the English edition was to be in four volumes. Since it was necessary for Carey to add a third volume, he had to cancel the title-pages of the first two volumes and correct the error on the printed boards of Volume I by means of a printed slip pasted over the error.

THE / FORTUNES OF NIGEL, /A Romance. /By the Author of Waverley, Ivanhoe, &c. /[rule] /Knifegrinder. Story? Lord bless you! I have none to tell, sir. /Poetry of the Anti-Jacobin. /[rule] /In Two Volumes. /Vol. I. [II.] /[double-rule] /Philadelphia: /H. C. Carey and I. Lea, Chestnut Street, /And /H. C. Carey & Co. Broadway, New York. /[line of seven dots] / 1822.

There happen to be no cancel leaves in the English edition of this novel, but as it is the one which first set afoot the present investigation, and as it has an interesting point, it is included here.

A copy of an odd Volume I of the American edition in contemporary calf which came to hand was tossed aside as imperfect, as it lacked the long "Epistle Introductory" which is in Volume I of the English edition. On examining another calf copy of the American edition of Volume I, the "Epistle" was noted as in the English edition, and it seemed that the binder had made a regrettable error in assembling the sheets of the Volume I first mentioned above.

Sometime later, a Volume II of the American edition was examined (a copy in original boards), and this too, contained the "Epistle Introductory." But the volume also contained a note on a slip pasted between the front cover and the fly-leaf:

To The Reader

The "Epistle Introductory" to this work was not received by the American publishers until after the first volume was printed and done up in boards. It is therefore prefixed to the second volume.

Gentlemen who may desire to have the volumes bound after reading them, can have the Epistle properly placed by giving instructions to this effect to the binders.
July 12, 1822.

It seemed odd at the time that Carey should have received the text proper without the introductory matter if he was printing from a copy of the English edition of the book. If, however, he had managed to get sheets, it was perfectly explicable, as preliminary matter is generally set up last in the printing of a book, and the Epistle Introductory would, therefore, be among the last of the sheets received. Further investigation, as detailed above, proved this original supposition correct. The quoted slip shows also that Carey worked fast when he received the precious sheets, and that his henchman in Ballantyne's shipped them on to him as they came off the press, and did not wait until the novel was completely finished before mailing. An efficient pair, evidently.

REDGAUNTLET. /A Tale of the Eighteenth Century. /By the Author of "Waverley." /[rule] /Master, go on; and I will follow thee, /To the last gasp, with truth and loyalty. /As You Like It. / [rule] /In Two Volumes. / Vol. I. [II.] /[double-rule] /Philadelphia: /H. C. Carey and I. Lea--Chestnut Street. / [row of ten dots] / 1824.

Worthington says: "The following leaves were cancelled: Vol. I, pp. 97-104 (G 1 to G 4), pp. 231-232 (P 4), and pp. 239-240 (P 8). Vol. III, pp. 71-72."

English First Edition	American, as above
Vol. I, pp. 97-104.	Vol. I, pp. 57-62. As this agrees with the reading of the English cancellans, it is obvious that in this instance Carey was sent revised sheets.
Vol. I, pp. 231-232. The Van Antwerp copy, which contains the cancellandum, shows the reason for cancellation was the addition of another character to the scene in the hall by adding "Dougal MacAllum" after "the Laird."	Vol. I, pp. 139-140. As above.
Vol. I, pp. 239-240. The Van Antwerp copy, which contains the cancellandum, shows the reason for cancellation was a slip of the pen, "Sir Robert" being printed for "Sir John."	Vol. I, pp. 144-145. As above.
Vol. III, page 71, line 16. *Bellerophontes.*	Vol. II, page 136, line 23. *Bellephontes.*

Carey printed the first two thirds of this novel from sheets which were sent him with the cancellans, and hence the American edition contains, for these volumes, the revised reading. The latter part of the novel, however (perhaps the last volume), reached him in uncorrected sheets, with the cancellandum, and hence the American edition shows the original misspelling, *Bellephontes* for *Bellerophontes*, which caused the cancel.

TALES / OF THE CRUSADERS. /By the Author of "Waverley," / "Quentin Durward," &c. /In Four Volumes. [rule] /Vol. III. [IV.] /The Talisman. /[double-rule] /Philadelphia: /H. C. Carey & I. Lea--Chestnut Street. /[rule] / 1825.

Worthington says: "Pages 125-126 (H 7) of Vol. III are a cancel in all the copies I have seen."

Pages 67-68, Vol. III, American edition above, present no differences from the cancellans in the English edition, i.e., Carey was working from revised sheets or from the printed book. Incidentally, Vols. I and II of the American and English editions contain *The Betrothed*, Vols. III and IV *The Talisman*. I have not seen the first two volumes with the Carey imprint.

ANNE OF GEIERSTEIN; /Or, /The Maiden of the Mist. /[rule] /By the Author of "Waverley." /[rule] /In Two Volumes. /Vol. I. [II.] /[double-rule] /Philadelphia: /Carey, Lea & Carey--Chestnut Street. /[rule]. 1829.

Worthington says: "Vol. II, pages 263-264 (L 12) are cancelled in all the copies I have seen."

English First Edition	American, as above
Vol. II, page 263, middle of line 15 to the end of the page:	Vol. II, pages 48-49, corresponding passage:
Fatigue at length prevailed over anxiety, and he fell into a deep and profound sleep, from which he was only awakened by returning light. He resolved on an instant departure from so dangerous a spot, and without seeing any one of the household but the old ostler, pursued his journey to Strasburg, and reached that city without further accident.	*Fatigue at length prevailed over anxiety, and he fell into a deep and profound sleep, in which state we will for the present leave him, to return to the fortunes of his son.*
	Note: Van Antwerp has compared the reading of the original MS in the Pierpont Morgan Library with the English cancellans and found other differences, errors which, as they were evidently corrected in the galley stage, do not appear in the American edition.

Vol. II, page 264, line 7 of   Vol. II, page 50, line 7 of
quotation: quotation:
  foliage.   *folliage.*

WOODSTOCK; /Or/THE CAVALIER. /A Tale /Of the Year /Sixteen
Hundred and Fifty-One. /[rule] /"He was a perfect gentle
Knight."--Chaucer. /[rule] /By the Author of "Waverley," Tales of
the /Crusaders, &c. &c. / In Two Volumes. /[rule] /Vol. I. [II.]
/Philadelphia: /H.C. Carey & I. Lea, Chestnut Street / 1826.

Worthington says: "The title-page of Vol. I is a cancel in all the
copies I have seen. Pages 168-169 (L 4) of Vol. III are also a
cancel. I have never seen this leaf uncancelled but it is found in
two different states after cancellation. The first has the figure '17'
at the foot of page 167 and an exclamation mark after the word
'orders' in line 16 of page 168. The other state has neither.
Although the evidence is not conclusive I believe the former to be
the earlier as there is no exclamation mark in the 'Author's Favorite
Edition.'"
  The American edition was evidently set up from revised
sheets, as there are no differences between the reading with the
English cancellans. Mr. Worthington's guess at the exclamation
mark is borne out by the American edition, however, as it does
have an exclamation mark after the word 'orders' (Vol. II, page
186, line 37).
  Van Antwerp gives the reason for the cancellation of the title-
page from a note to the printer on the corrected title-page in the
Pierpont Morgan Library: Scott had intended the sub-title to be "A
Tale of Long Parliament Times."
  The American edition, however, contains an error which may
have been the cause of a re-cancellation of the English title-page,
or may merely be an American printer's error. The legend on the
title-page in the English edition reads, correctly, "He was a very
perfect gentle knight." In the American edition the quotation is
given, incorrectly, "He was a perfect gentle knight." The line is 72
in the *Prologue* of *The Canterbury Tales*, "He was a very parfit
gentil knight."
  It would be interesting to know if the word *very* was in the
original English title-page, for, if it were not, Scott would certainly
have ordered a cancellation.

Incidentally, the American edition has commas after the words *mazy* and *entered*--(page 167, line 12, and page 168, line 4, respectively). The commas do not appear in the English edition.

CHRONICLES / OF /THE CANONGATE; /By /The Author of "Waverley," &c. /[rule] /Sic Itur Ad Astra. /Motto of the Canongate Arms. /[rule] /In Two Volumes. /Vol. I. [II.] /[double-rule] /Philadelphia: /Carey, Lea & Carey--Chestnut Street. /[rule] / 1827.

Worthington says: "Vol. I, pages 203-204 (N 6), are a cancel in some copies. In the original state of this leaf, line 2 of page 203 begins with the word *it*. Vol. II, pages 63-64 and 65-66 (D 8 and E 1) are both cancels. Two states of these leaves are found. When D 8 is uncancelled, line 15 of page 63 begins with the word *wretch* (in italics).

"E 1 is always a cancel, but also exists in two states, the first being identified by the fifth word in line 16 on page 66, which is *care.*

"For some reason, however, D 8 was also cancelled, and E 1 was re-cancelled. The two leaves were then printed together and inserted conjugate. In this form line 15 of page 63 begins *retch* and the fifth word in line 16 or page 66 in now *charge.*"

Van Antwerp says, and correctly: "The text of the Waverley Novels presents many bibliographical problems, and nowhere are these more baffling than in the first Series of the 'Chronicles of the Canongate.'" After giving Worthington's statements, he says further: "I own three copies; in two of them there are no cancels whatever; in my third copy pages 65-66 (E 1), of Vol. II, alone is cancelled. Each of the leaves to which Mr. Worthington refers is printed exactly alike in all three of my copies and each conforms to his identification of the first state. It is very puzzling."

English First Edition	American, as above
Vol. I, page 204, lines 10-11, *"Yes," she added, with a wild shriek, "murdered your mother's fathers in their peaceful dwelling,"* etc.	Vol. I, page 158, line 25, *"Murdered your mother's parents."*

Vol. I, page 204, lines 14-15,
 *"I attended to the voice of my
 mother--well I remember her
 words!--They came in peace,"* etc.

Vol. I, page 158, lines 28-30,
 *"I attended to the voice of
 my mother--but I can
 remember, they came in
 peace,"* etc.

Vol. II, page 63, line 15,
 "wretch."

Vol. II, page 45, line 32,
 Same reading as the
 English edition.

Vol. II, page 65, line 7-8,
 *Zilia de Moncada heard the
 question, (which, being
 addressed to the father, Grey
 had inconsiderately uttered in
 French), and it seemed as if,* etc.

Vol. II, page 46, lines 35-37,
 *Zilia de Moncada heard the
 question; and it seemed as
 if,* etc.
 Note: The error in this
 sentence, which Scott
 caught and corrected in the
 English edition, lies in the
 fact that a few paragraphs
 earlier it had been stated that
 Zilia de Moncada
 "understands no English."

CHRONICLES / OF / THE CANONGATE. /Second Series. / By /The Author of "Waverley," &c. /[rule] /Sic Itur Ad Astra. /Motto of the Canongate Arms. /[rule] /In Two Volumes. /Vol. I [II.] /[double-rule] /Philadelphia: /Carey, Lea and Carey--Chestnut Street. /[rule] / 1828.

There are no cancels in the English edition of this volume, but it is of some interest, however, in a comparison of labels.

English edition labels

American edition labels

Chronicles / Of The / Canongate.
/ Second Series. / By The /
Author of / Waverley, &c. / [rule]
/ In Three Vols. / [rule] / Vol. I.
[II. III.] /

[Double-rule] / St. Valentine's
/ Day; / Or The / Fair Maid /
Of Perth. / By The / Author /
Of / Waverley. / [rule] /
Vol. I. [II.] / [double-rule] /

Scott had intended titling the novel as the American edition labels read, but changed his mind at the last moment. It is probable that the American edition title-pages (which are cancellans in every copy I have seen) were originally printed as the labels.

TALES OF MY LANDLORD, / Fourth and Last Series, / Collected and Arranged / By / Jedediah Cleishbotham, / Schoolmaster and Parish-Clerk of Gandercleugh. / [rule] / [eight line quotation from Robert Burns] / [rule] / In Three Volumes. / Vol. I. [II. III.] / [double-rule] / Philadelphia: / Carey and Lea--Chestnut Street. / [rule] / 1832.

Volumes II and III have a six line quotation from *Don Juan* (which occurs on the title-pages of the first three volumes of the English edition, the final volume only bearing the eight line Burns quotation), and the variant imprint Philadelphia: / Carey & Lea. / [rule] / 1832.

The arrangement of the American edition differs considerably from the English edition, probably because of the order in which the sheets were received by Carey. The English edition is in four volumes--Volume I containing the Introduction and *Count Robert of Paris*, Volume II continuing *Count Robert*, Volume III concluding *Count Robert* and containing also the beginning of *Castle Dangerous*, and Volume IV concluding *Castle Dangerous* and ending with the Author's Note, dated Abbotsford, September, 1831.

The American edition is in three volumes, Volume I containing the Introduction and *Castle Dangerous*, and Volumes II and III containing *Count Robert of Paris*, following which is the Author's Note as above.

Worthington says: "The following leaves were cancelled in all the copies I have seen: Vol. I, pages 91-92 (d 10), and pages 97-98 (E 1). Vol. II, pages 143-144 (f 12)." Van Antwerp does not mention the cancels.

English First Edition	American, as above
Vol. I, page 92, lines 7-11, read	Vol. II, page 53, lines 2-5,

as follows:

One goodly old man, named Michael Agelastes, big, burly, and dressed like an ancient Cynic philosopher, was distinguished by assuming, in a great measure, the rugged garb and mad bearing of that sect, etc.

Same page, line 24.

Elephans.

Vol. I, page 97, lines 13-14, read as follows:

The language was Saxon which these foreigners occasionally used.

Vol. II, page 144, lines 17-20, read as follows:

She had resented her separation from her husband, and committed some violence upon the slaves of the Household.

read as follows:

One goodly old man, named Michael Agelastes, big, burly, and dressed like an ancient Cynic philosopher, was distinguished by assuming, in a great manner, the rugged garb and mad bearing of the stoic, etc.

Same page, line 16.

Elephantos.

Vol. II, page 55, lines 15-16, read as follows:

The language was Saxon which these foreigners always used.

Vol. II, page 209, lines 13-15, read as follows:

She had resented her separation from her husband, and committed some violence upon the slaves of the Haram.

NOTES

[1]For an enlightening essay on this whole subject, from which the above examples are taken, see "Sir Walter Scott and His Literary Rivals in the Old South," by Grace Warren Landrum in *American Literature*, November, 1930. See also "America's Tragedy," by James Truslow Adams (New York, 1935), pp. 95, 119, 129, 339, 340.

[2]Collection of Papers of Archibald Constable & Co., National Library of Scotland, MS 791, p. 537.

[3]See Henry Charles Lea: A Biography. By Edward Sculley Bradley. Philadelphia. University of Pennsylvania Press, 1931.

[4]In the following discussion of cancels I must make clear my indebtedness to R. W. Chapman's *Cancels*, one of the Sadleir *Bibliographia Series* (London, 1930). This work is indispensable to a study of the subject. The collector of Scott will appreciate my indebtedness, too, to Greville Worthington's *A Bibliography of the Waverley Novels*, in the same series (1931), and to William C. Van Antwerp's *A Collector's Comments on His First Editions of the Works of Sir Walter Scott* (San Francisco, 1932).

10

FOOTNOTE ON A MINOR POET (1938)

Randall adds considerably to what little was known about this "minor poet," William Wilberforce Lord. A victim of Edgar Allan Poe's criticism, Lord nevertheless had several important connections in American literary circles. [From *The Colophon, A Quarterly for Bookmen*, New Series, 3 (Autumn, 1938): 587-597.]

Of all the minor poets of the nineteenth century, few were so completely forgotten by succeeding generations as William Wilberforce Lord. His first book, *Poems*, was published in 1845; his second, *Christ in Hades*, in 1851; his third--and last--*Andre*, in 1857. Although the author lived until 1907, none of his works achieved republication until twenty-five years after his death. His very name was known only to those students of American literature who study the Poe minutiae, and yet few first volumes of poetry were so eagerly looked for as his own, few were preceded by such extravagant praise, and few so bitterly received or so speedily forgotten.

In 1938, due to the growing consciousness on the part of Americans in their literary tradition, his works were collected and edited by Professor Thomas Ollive Mabbott and issued in a handsome volume by Random House. Unfortunately, little seems to be known about Lord's early life and Professor Mabbott did not have access to the letters which are quoted here. In view of Lord's early promise and his unfortunate treatment at the hands of Edgar Allan Poe, it may be that details of the publication of his works, as recounted in his letters, will be of interest.

William Wilberforce Lord was born October 28, 1814, in Madison County, New York, of the seventh generation in America of both sides of the family. According to Griswold, failing health while in college caused him to embark on that early nineteenth century panacea for all ills, a whaling voyage, and there is some reason to believe that he sailed in the same vessel which had earlier carried R. H. Dana, Jr., on his journey immortalized in *Two Years Before The Mast*. Upon his return Lord entered Auburn Theological Seminary and later, in 1843, Princeton Theological Seminary, from which he was graduated in 1845.

It was while he was at Princeton that he began writing poems which so impressed his friends (who included Charles Fenno Hoffman and Charles King) that they insisted he publish them. Indeed they praised him so highly, referring to him in print--and before he had published almost anything--as the "American Milton," that it seems doubtful if anything Lord could have produced would have satisfied the public's expectations.

Late in 1844 or early in 1845 he met the well-known publicist and writer W. Burnet Kinney, the founder, and at that time the editor, of the *Newark Daily Advertiser*. Kinney's wife, Elizabeth Clementine Dodge Stedman Kinney, by her first marriage the mother of Edmund Clarence Stedman, was a poet and essayist of considerable reputation. Lord was immediately welcomed into the Kinney circle, and it is a part of his recently recovered correspondence with them which is printed here.

Mr. Kinney undertook to aid Lord in issuing his book, and Lord at one time thought of dedicating it to Mrs. Kinney and indeed wrote her a dedicatory poem which was finally published at the end of the volume under the title *L'Envoi*. Included in the volume (which was eventually dedicated to Professor Albert A. Dod of Princeton, through whom Lord had made the Kinney's acquaintance) is a sonnet to Mr. Kinney.

Early in 1845 (Lord dated little of his early correspondence, so the arrangement is problematical) he wrote the following letters to his patrons:

"Princeton, Tuesday.

"Your announcement that Mr. Appleton did not wish to produce the Book until Spring evoked up my Familiar, the Daemon, I mean, of Poesy, or frenzy or whatever it is that inhabits me, with the suggestion that I might complete my Mosaic drama and bring it out with the collection. The possibility of this, however, depends (that is, if the price of the Book is fixed at what you stated) on the probability that you have misconceived its size. Professor Dod stated to you that the manuscript contained three thousand lines, this was a mistake. They do not contain, as I think, over two thousand lines. So you see that if Mr. A. made his calculation in view of three thousand, then there would be room for the drama. The time is short indeed for a well-considered composition of the thing, but my conception of it is clear and I feel confident that I could accomplish it. Tell me what you think of the plan. If decided upon, the drama must come in at the end in order not to interrupt the printing of the other poems, and the Hebrew Hymn and many choruses which are parts of it must be struck out of the list of contents. L'Envoi, of course, will close the Book as before intended."

(Extract from another letter to Mrs. Kinney.)
    "Everybody, that is, the few bodies who interest themselves in me, are very impatient for the Book. It has certainly been delayed too long. Seeing that the Gazette (U.S.) and Chas. King have exposed me so prematurely, the book should not be delayed a moment longer than necessary.
    ". . . Mr. Kinney ought to tell the publishers that he must have the proofs today and send the revise to me tomorrow, or next day. I am heartily sorry--almost ashamed of the trouble I give him in this matter, which you have sometimes spoken of, but he never. However if he will think the Book poetry, he undoubtedly has a reward in the labour independently of my gratitude."

"(Mr. K.)
"Princeton, Feb. 10.
    "I send within the promised communications. If you have not been to New York yet, perhaps it would be best to place the poem of the defeat of Henry Clay in the collection. A suitable place for it would be immediately before the Ode on the Present Crisis.[1] The title must be 'On the Defeat of a Great Man.' The piece is already known to have been intended for Mr. Clay. And the generalization 'Great Man' will only add to the effect of the special application which cannot fail to be made."

"(Mrs. K.)
"March 9.
    "You--that is Mr. K. speaks of sending the proof sheets of the
Ode to England to Mr., beg the Right Reverend's pardon, Bishop
Doane to forward to Wordsworth. I vehemently desire that he
would send the Worship also. If transmitted through Appleton he
might not only send that, also Niagara and the Sky."

"Princeton, Monday.
"My dear K.
    "Dr. Hodge and Theo Ledyard Cuyler both mistook the New
Castalia for a serious attempt. Dr. Hodge was quite certain that it
would be mistaken by most and was very anxious that it should be
explained in a note or otherwise. What do you think of appending
a note--thus Appendix.[2]

Note 1

Page . . . . etc.

    "New Castalia. As several of the Author's friends have
mistaken this playful imitation of a modern style of versification for
an obscure (or) allegorical attempt at something, he thought it best
to adopt the advice of Nick to Snug and tell them plainly he is no
lion."

    About the middle of May, 1845, Appleton issued the book,
modestly entitled *Poems*, and Edgar Allan Poe reviewed it for the
May 24th issue of the newly-founded *Broadway Journal* partly as
follows:

Of Mr. Lord we know nothing--although we believe that he is a
student in Princeton College--or perhaps a graduate or perhaps a
Professor of that institution. Of his book lately we have heard a
great deal--that is to say, we have heard it announced in every
possible variation of praise, as was forthcoming. . .
    The fact is that the only remarkable thing about Mr. Lord's
compositions are their remarkable conceit, ignorance, impudence,
platitude, stupidity and bombast. . .

    This was just the beginning, and Poe went on to accuse Lord
of plagiarism and bad grammar, and concluded with "Good Lord
Deliver Us." All in all it was a devastating review, and the more

cutting to Lord because it was entirely undeserved. For Poe was attacking not Lord, but his sponsors. True, Lord's *New Castalia* was a burlesque of *The Raven*, and Poe had quarreled with one of his best friends for writing a parody on *The Haunted Palace*. But more important, Lord's sponsors were partisans of the *Knickerbocker Magazine*, which was engaged in a literary war with Poe, and so in his review, as Professor Mabbott points out, Poe "was fighting effectively and criticizing execrably."

Of course Lord was hurt by the review, but he was not killed by a bad press any more than Keats was. On May 28, 1845, he writes to Mrs. Kinney:

"If I were to write my heart to you now it would only be a repetition of L'Envoi. I thought Poe's attack worth answering only on account of the charge of plagiarism. Some of his specifications are ludicrous enough. The Lenore and Al Araaf, as I think he calls it, I never saw. That he should charge me with stealing the croaks of his Raven for the New Castalia and at the same time perceive it to be a satire is surprising. I assure you that I bate no jot of heart or hope. My fate is not dependent upon the success of that book though my temporal and temporary condition must necessarily be very much affected by it. Mr. Poe must have read the book with great care to have culled all its solecisms (which are blunderings of the press), together with the cases of verbal license, justifiable, although he does not seem to know it, by authority. Mr. Hoffman in his talented and manly critique speaks to my consciousness in what he says of the bookish character of the poems with the exception (I think) of Worship and Niagara. The poems seem esoterically, as I learn from many quarters, to have met with great success.

'It is evident that there was too much noise made about the book before its appearance. My book (like this) apotheosized in anticipation is certain likewise to be damned in anticipation. . .

"When shall I see you. I have a growing aversion since my notoriety to going abroad, that is, where I am known. I received a letter yesterday from Cuyler which is quite enthusiastic and highly indignant at the attack in the B[roadway] J[ournal] which he says is exposed for sale in Boston at the Bookstores. It has been sent here likewise in considerable quantities and has been placed gratuitously in our Reading Room. . ."

By June, however, Lord was again upset by what he considered the publisher's lack of dignity, and on the 11th he writes Mrs. Kinney:

"The book is unfortunate in several particulars but its chief misfortune is that it is poetry, the first attempt at which if successful has always been esteemed a capital crime. Secondarily it is marred by such faults as a first book of verse by an unpracticed writer--a book whose subject matter was conceived, embodied and put forth in the space of a few months might be expected to exhibit. But finally, it was ushered into the world with too many notes of preparation--some of which indeed were given with no uncertain sound through trumpets of divinely tempered alchemy while others bore a distinct resemblance to the tintinnabulations of jingled cow bells. And superfluously, or as Willis would say, whose notice, by the by, was the best I have seen corollarily, the publishers forgetting that modesty is always the best claim to notice, pushed the book in the most vulgar manner. I blush to the tips of my fingers while I record the first 'notice' that I saw of the book was contained in the publisher's bill upon a bookseller's door in which I saw the letters of my own name standing like ill-assorted columns and endeavoring to hide themselves under the startling entablature 'CHOICE AMERICAN POETRY.' Ye Powers! To swear by no profaner oath. Do not wonder that I forget my clerical character, a saint might have blasphemed, but blasphemy would not have expressed the anger of an irascible sinner like myself when I saw this execrable piece of cockneyism and stupidity.

"But enough of this. I long to see you and our mutual lover my dear K. I fear that his sensitiveness which is far greater than mine must have been severely wounded, when mine has received so rude a shock. . .

"As ever yours,
"W.W.L.

"P.S. I received the Alleghanian and saw the notice in the Commercial."

And still more heartache was coming to Lord. Bishop Doane had, as promised, shown the poems to Wordsworth, who thought highly of them. His kind words after the book's reception in his own country must have been balm to Lord's tortured nerves, and understandably enough the young poet wrote to his publisher and told him what the master had said (Mabbott's Introduction to the 1938 edition of Lord's *Poems*, p. ix):

"Mr. Appleton:
"Dear Sir: Your interest in my little venture upon the high seas of literature, especially since it has met with some adverse winds, will perhaps rate a piece of intelligence, that you will have no doubt gratified me in some degree, gratifying to you. I have been favoured with a communication from Bishop Doane which contains the following extract from a letter to him by William Wordsworth. ('I have to thank you for several specimens of the abilities of a young poet, which seem to me of high promise. They are full of deep emotion, and not wanting in vigorous and harmonious expression. Pray convey to him my best wishes for his health and happiness and success in that department of literature in which it becomes every day more difficult to obtain and secure attention, however well it may be deserved.')

"I shall be happy to hear from you and learn something of the prospects of the Book.

"Your ob't s'v't, W.W.Lord."

Professor Mabbott comments: "The words of Wordsworth seem to have been inserted in the newspapers at the time, though we have not met with any copy of them hitherto in print." They were inserted in the *New York Tribune*,[3] and immediately poor Lord, more heartbroken than by Poe's attack, wrote to Mrs. Kinney (September 18, 1845):

"Princeton, Thur. Sept. 18, 1845
"Mr dear E.B.K.:
"I am sick at heart this morning--not in the common sense. I am not mad, that is, nor melancholy, but I have a fever of the spirit upon me. These Appletons will be the death of me. Another piece of stupid and senseless vulgarity from them and Shame will be ashamed to be my fellow. Another of their attempts to bring me into notice and Charon will not ferry me over the River Styx. Do you know that the extract from Wordsworth's letter, which I communicated to them privately, and supposed that they would make dignified and cautious use of--Oh 'mea culpa' not to be

taught by experience--would you believe that they have thrown it into a common sewer, have cast it under the 'hoofs of the swinish multitude'--have--Gods and Demons!--have given it to the New York Tribune to be circulated like an advertisement of Blackings. I wrote to Bishop Doane this morning to let him know that I had no part in it. I expressed my feeling of mortification that the extract (which as Mr. Kinney knows I did not wish published at all) should have appeared in such an organ. Nor does it, I told him in conclusion, at all alleviate the feeling to know that two esteemed and venerable names have been connected with one so insignificant as my own, in a print whose notice is, so far, a title to contempt, and whose praises would make fame look like infamy."

So ends the story of the first publication of one who had been hailed "the American Milton." Lord says no more about the book in his letters to the Kinneys. He did some lecturing around New York in 1846 and at Amherst in 1847, and in 1848 was ordained deacon in the Protestant Episcopal Church and ordained priest by Bishop Doane in 1850. During these years he saw little of the Kinneys, although he corresponded with them. In 1850 Mr. Kinney was appointed charge d'affaires at Sardinia, and from 1850 to 1853 they resided in Turin. In 1853, the Sardinian mission having ended, they moved to Florence, where they lived for more than ten years and were members of the famous circle which included the Brownings, the Tennysons, and the Trollopes.

Lord did not forget them, however, nor did they cease to aid him, for on September 27, 1850, he writes Mrs. Kinney about his second book:[4]

"I have put my poem to press with the agreement that, if at the end of the year it does not sell enough to pay expenses, Mr. Appleton is to notify me and in case of my disability rely upon Mr. Kinney's guarantee. These are the best terms I could make with him. He seems, however, to expect it not only to pay but to remunerate. I have taken the liberty of dedicating it to Mr. Kinney, I hope it will gratify him--at least that he will not think it an unwarrantable freedom in one, who in doing this only consults his heart.

"This is the form of the Dedication. I have avoided, you will perceive, all commonplace expressions of consideration, etc., but I think it all the more significant:

To
William B. Kinney, Esq.
With the hope that his judgment
will approve a work, to the fate of
which friendship will not permit him to
be indifferent, this Poem is
Inscribed by the
Author.

"I have read the Preface and the last book to Bishop Whittingham and he expressed himself as not having a doubt of its success."

Early in January, 1851, he again writes Mrs. Kinney:

"I have for a long time delayed writing in the hope that I should soon be able to send you my book. I send the Preface and Invocation. And Thomas will send the book so soon as published. I am called to a Parish in Maryland and shall not be here to see it myself. . .

"You will perceive by the proof sheets I send that I have improved the wording (of the Dedication)[5] somewhat. Mr. Griswold is confident that the Book will go.

"My dear E.C.K. if even five or ten years from now the book should have obtained an established reputation--how grateful will be the thought that it was through the means of my dearest earthly friends that it saw the light, and that I laid it--with whatever of promise and auspicious features it then wore--at their feet."

In 1854 Lord became rector of Christ's Church at Vicksburg, Mississippi. He was an intimate friend of Jefferson Davis, became a well-known educator, and during the Civil War was chaplain of the first Mississippi Brigade. During the siege of Vicksburg his library, which was reputed to be the largest and most scholarly in the south, was destroyed. Just after moving to Vicksburg, however, he wrote his last published poetry: *Andre: A Tragedy in Five Acts* (New York: Charles Scribner's Sons, 1856). And from Vicksburg he writes Mrs. Kinney, March 16, 1857:

"Your critique of my Andre in the Newark Daily Advertiser, if grateful to my feelings as an author was still more gratifying to me as a friend. . . . I am almost as remote from our old paradise of the Poets which bloomed so freely in mechanical Newark, as you are. I am the rector of a considerable Parish in the inconsiderable city of Vicksburg on the bank of the Mississippi. . . . On the whole I am happy. I have ceased to expect anything from my contemporaries but the respectful damnation of faint praise. I published my Andre because having been recently twice very near death, once by the Yellow Fever and once by a fall from a horse, I was reminded that my poem ran the same risk."

The Civil War came, the Kinneys stayed abroad, and their correspondence lapsed. Not until a score of years later did Mrs. Kinney and W. W. Lord correspond again. Then, in the late 70's Lord was called to Christ's Church, Cooperstown, New York, and there, Mrs. Kinney's son, Edmund Clarence Stedman called upon him. In 1881 (July 11) Lord wrote Mrs. Kinney one of his last letters:

"I have read the Victorian poets with great interest. The most striking feature of the book is the space allotted and the justice done the minor poets, who should be called, rather, the minus poets: viz: before whom the reading public, or more likely the writing, have put the sign of indeterminate value. Thus while $+100$ means 100, -100 may mean much less or much more. Its value depends on its relations to other symbols and figures unexpressed. The great English donkey (I speak of the genus) so prolific of genius in individuals, wrote '-' against the name of William Shakespeare and '+' before that of Ben Jonson, as at another period of its history, '-' before John Milton and '+' before John Dryden. 'But the whirligig of time brings in its revenges.'

"How can you be sensitive on account of my failure to speak of your Poems, for which let me thank you. Did we not long ago agree with each other that we were poets, Arcades ambo? And now you are the poet-mother of a famous poet-son. And I have attained only to the first condition of fame--detraction."

NOTES

[1]It was not so placed.

[2]This note was not printed.

[3]September 17, 1845.

[4]*Christ in Hades.* New York, D. Appleton and Co., 1851.

[5]The changes are: "To Hon. William B. Kinney," not "To William B. Kinney, Esq." and the omission of the words "the fate of" as quoted above.

11

A PLEA FOR A MORE CONSISTENT POLICY OF CATALOGUING BY AUCTION GALLERIES (1946)

This sobering survey of American book auction cataloguing practices, based upon sales during 1945, was presented at the January 18, 1946, meeting of the Bibliographical Society of America. [From *Papers of the Bibliographical Society of America*, 40 (Second Quarter, 1946): 107-126.]

T HE back page of The [London] *Times Literary Supplement* is occasionally devoted to bibliographical matters, collations of books, reports on auction sales, etc. It is a matter of regret, incidentally, that no American literary magazine devotes any considerable space to such concerns. In the issue of July 28, 1945, its correspondent, in reporting the results of the Frank J. Hogan sale of English literature, has some remarks upon the cataloguing of one of the items: "Auctioneers' licence, in the United States at least, is considerable and this description cannot pass at its face value." "Moreover, although the auction catalogue quotes such other portions of the letter as may enhance its attraction in the eyes of a distant buyer, it not only omits part of it vital to the proper estimation of its standing but adds an editorial note to another section quoted from it the effect of which can be no other than the falsification of the whole purport of the letter." "With the effect on the price of the item we have little to do; its prejudicial effect on bibliographical research is another matter; . . ." For another item: "As the cataloguer dislikes the implication of the word 'second' he retains the 'large paper,'" and so on.

Now I have no comments to make upon the correctness of *The Times* correspondent's particular strictures.[a] What is disquieting to me, however, is the knowledge that, in general, his assertion that "auctioneers' licence, in the United States at least, is considerable" has a large measure of truth. The erratic cataloguing of books of importance by auction houses has been a matter of comment, at least in private conversations, among American collectors, librarians and dealers for quite some time. *The Times* article merely brought the matter into the open.

Generally speaking the various galleries have been lax in their cataloguing, occasionally flatly contradicting in one catalogue what has recently been said in another, quoting as freely from outdated or discredited bibliographies as from reliable ones, frequently neglecting current and up-to-date information, making invalid statements on insufficient evidence, and making no apparent effort to maintain a standardized bibliographical nomenclature. Now this is, or should be of considerable concern to collectors, librarians and dealers who have a right to expect a higher standard of bibliographical accuracy in descriptions than they have recently been getting. If this seems a rather harsh indictment of our auction houses, I beg indulgence of judgment until the record is partially examined. The record for the purposes of this paper deals largely with auction catalogues issued in 1945, deals chiefly with English and American literature, does not touch upon any bibliographical information which is not a matter of public record, and is concerned chiefly with American sources of information.

Let us consider first the matter of contradictions: In the recent Clemens sales a "large paper" copy of Pope's *The Dunciad* (Dublin Printed, London Reprinted for A. Dodd, 1728) was catalogued as *both* "octavo" and "duodecimo on large paper" and as "First or Second Edition" with the note: "Although Dublin appears in the imprint, the book was printed in London and no Dublin edition was every printed. Cf. Griffith, Nos. 198-199."[1] Three months later the Hogan copy, octavo and also on large paper, immediately became: "The exceedingly rare first issue of the first edition" and in the note was the statement: "The work was published in both London and Dublin in 1728 - each edition, for the sake of obscurity, professing to be a reprint of the other. Cf. the catalogue of the Rowfant Library, p. 164."[2] There is no need to go into the tangled bibliography of this work, a subject of speculation since 1854, but a reading of the two entries is instructive. The cataloguer states, in the Hogan description: "Dr. Wise refutes Professor Griffith's doubts more or less conclusively and has found general agreement."

In the Bronson Winthrop sale, March, 1945, his copy of Pope's *Essay on Man* (London [1733]) was catalogued: "Each part is the correct first issue according to Griffith's generally accepted conclusions,"[3] Part I being noted as Griffith 294, Epistle II Griffith 300, Epistle III Griffith 308. Yet when the Hogan copy came up the next month, Part I being Griffith 304, it was catalogued as "considered by many bibliographers the first issue"[4] (though not by Griffith, whose conclusions had been "generally accepted" the previous month in making the Winthrop copy "the correct first issue of each part"). And Epistles II and III, still Griffith 300 and 308, are catalogued with the note, in each case: "Griffith is doubtful;" "Griffith was in doubt."

Or consider the "New York Collector's" copy of Boswell's *Life of Johnson* (London, 1791). This is catalogued as ". . . page 135, Vol. I, is in the first state with the reading 'gve' in line 10."[5] Leaving aside the highly dubious bibliographical accuracy of this statement, how did the same Galleries catalogue the other variant the last time they had it? As, logically they should have: "second state"? Not at all. The note to the Clemens copy simply said: "with the word 'give' correctly spelled on page 135, Vol. I."[6] One other example of this type of cataloguing will suffice. In the Newton sale Conrad and Hueffer's *The Inheritors* (London, 1901) is catalogued perfectly correctly as "First English Edition. First Issue before the dedication leaf was added,"[7] etc. But the Hogan copy of the second issue is catalogued simply as "First English Edition. With the dedication leaf pasted in,"[8] etc. No "second issue" is mentioned. Now I do not ask that the words "second issue" be printed in the capital letters that the words "first issue" usually are, but I do think that, even if in lower case, they should be present.

It is quite a feat to reverse oneself within the limits of a single description, but as evidence that it can be done, witness the following: In a mixed sale of November 6, 1944, there was a collection of Latin poems catalogued under the heading, "The First

Book Printed at Vilna." The imprint is given as Vilna, 1573, and beneath all this is the note: "It seems that this book was printed in Germany and not in Vilna as printing was not introduced there before 1580."[9]

A delightful, if somewhat extreme, example of befuddlement occurred in the Clemens sale where Gray's *Odes* is catalogued as "Printed at Strawberry-Hill, for R. and J. Dodsley, 1757. . . . First Edition. Printed on thick paper." A few lines further on is the note: "The most sensational forgery that Mr. Hazen has so far discovered is none other than the thick paper 'Odes' which, although dated 1757, cannot, according to the evidence now discovered have been printed before about 1790."[10]

Again, it would seem hazardous to the average bibliographer to differentiate issues on the strength of a facsimile. But look at the description of Beaumont and Fletcher's *The Knight of the Burning Pestle* (London, 1635), with Beamount on the title-page-- catalogued as: "Probably the earlier of the two issues which appeared in 1635; the other has Beaumont's name spelled in the usual way,"[11] it being admitted in the description that the first three leaves of the copy described (which include the title-page) were in type facsimile.

This is no place to go into the merits of the "follow the flag" argument in collecting. But let's have a little consistency in whatever decision is taken. If it is decided to catalogue Twain's *The Adventures of Huckleberry Finn* (New York, 1885) as it has recently been consistently catalogued: "First American Edition, issued a few days after the English edition,"[12] one would logically expect in the same catalogue, *The Adventures of Tom Sawyer* (Hartford, 1876), which was issued six months after the English edition, to be catalogued similarly as "First American Edition,"[13] but of course it isn't. There is no need to labor this point of which dozens of examples could be quoted. And, while speaking of *Huckleberry Finn*, admittedly a difficult book bibliographically, the rather startling statement that the "first issue" has the "folio number on page 155 lacking,"[14] advanced recently, does not seem to have met with general acceptance.

There is no consistency either in the use of such terms as "first separate edition," "first collected edition," "issue," "impression," etc. Why is the Boston, 1870 edition of Aldrich's *Story of a Bad Boy* catalogued in the Clemens sale as "First

Separate Edition"?[15] Because it had previously appeared serially in *Young Folk's Magazine*? If so then hundreds of other books, for example, *Uncle Tom's Cabin*, or *A Farewell to Arms*, should in their book appearances be described as "First Separate Edition," as they had previously appeared in serial publication. But they aren't. In the Clemens sale Coleridge's *Sibylline Leaves* (London, 1817), is "First Edition"[16] while in Sale 517 it is "First Collected Edition."[17] In the Hogan sale, Franklin's *Cato Major* (with corrected spelling "only," page 27, line 5) is "second impression."[18] In the "New York Collector's" sale the same variant is "second issue."[19]

Now there are numerous cases of books with unsolved bibliographical problems where it is perfectly reasonable to state which variant is offered for sale without assigning priority. This is the present custom, at one auction house with, for example, Poe's *Tales*, 1845,[20] Longfellow's *Evangeline*,[21] and Galsworthy's *The Man of Property*.[22] That is all right with me although bibliographical evidence for assigning priority in each case is, I think, crystal clear. But the use of weasel words in many descriptions might be curtailed. "Believed to be" and "apparently in original size," for example. The Clemens copy of Shelley's *Adonais* in the original blue wrappers, uncut, is "apparently in the original size,"[23] and his *Epipsychidion*, "stitched, uncut and unopened" is also "apparently in the original size."[24] I would like to see a book stitched, uncut and unopened which was not in original size.

Worse even are the "believed to be's," coinciding as they do with an apparent assumption that American book auction records began in 1916. Byron's *Fare Thee Well!* in the Clemens sale[25] is a typical example. The description quotes Wise, who states (among other things) that J. A. Spoor owned the Henry Huth copy. The cataloguer himself admits that Spoor had no copy, let alone Huth's. There is no evidence (other than Wise's word) that Huth ever had one either! This "build-up" suspiciously follows the usual Wise procedure made familiar by Miss Ratchford's *Letters of Thomas J. Wise to John Henry Wrenn: A Further Inquiry into the Guilt of Certain Nineteenth Century Forgers* (New York, Alfred A. Knopf, 1945). It is interesting to note that the astute editor, Colton Storm, of the 1945 edition of *American Book-Prices Current*, has seen fit to enter this item with the note: "Apparently first edition, but see catalogue description." I protest, in this connection, against quoting "Dr." Wise's opinions and prejudices on bibliographical matters of importance. I am convinced that no single statement of Wise's, which stands on his own unsupported word, should be accepted without rigid examination. And I object particularly to information being lifted bodily from his bibliographies without any indication of its source. Dr. Robert M. Smith in his recent *The Shelley Legend* (New York, 1945) agrees, for in speaking of Wise's *Shelley Bibliography*, he states (p. 290): ". . . . neither the bibliographical descriptions nor transcriptions. . . can be relied upon; and the student is hereby warned not to accept any (of Wise's) bibliographical statements without independent checking."

The *Cambridge Bibliography of English Literature* (*vide* Dryden) states: "T.J. Wise's bibliographical statements must be accepted with caution." And Roland Baughman, in addressing the group on bibliographical evidence at the Modern Language Association at Chicago last month (December 27, 1945), warns very clearly that Wise's tampering with genuine books must receive a very great deal of attention from bibliographers before we may comfortably sit back and assume that his operations have been adequately uncovered and dealt with. And it is time, indeed long past time, to begin cataloguing the Wise fabrications, when they appear, as fabrications and not merely with the innocuous statement: "see Carter and Pollard." Only once, to my knowledge, has a gallery catalogued a book as a Wise forgery and then it was not a forgery. This happened recently when Mrs. Browning's *A Song*, Privately Printed, 1907, is listed as "Apparently one of the 'Wise Forgeries'" and with the statement: "This dubious leaflet is not listed in Carter and Pollard."[26] Why, may I ask, should it be? It is perfectly genuine and one of Wise's almost innumerable printings for private circulation which do not pretend to be other than what they are, perfectly respectable and honest and all properly listed in Partington's *Forging Ahead*, pp. 287, etc.

But back to Byron and *Fare Thee Well!* The description is headed: "We believe this is the first appearance at public sale of this excessively rare leaflet," and in the body of the note is the remark: "We were also unable to find a record of a copy having been sold at auction in consulting the indexes of the *American Book Prices Current* back to 1916." Byron's *Poems on Various Occasions* (Newark, 1807) is catalogued: "Apparently only one other copy has appeared at auction in this country--the August Leigh copy, which was first sold in the E.K. Butler sale and later fetched $3,000 in the Jerome Kern sale."[27] And this despite the fact that Spoor[28] had a copy, another was sold in 1935[29] and others in 1911[30] and 1912.[31]

Now what makes 1916 a year of decision in American book-collecting history? Why, if no copy can be located since that date, do some auction houses "believe no copy has ever occurred at auction sale"? American Book-Prices Current has turned the half-century mark now. It was born in 1894. Complete runs since then are available without too much effort if one cares to consult them. Why is only the past twenty-eight years of its existence of importance in deciding if, or if not, a book, has, or has not, "appeared before at public sale"? It cannot be that there were no important sales before 1916--that would rule out Chamberlain, Foote, Hoe, and others too numerous to mention. Suppose, for example, a copy of The Bay Psalm Book was to be sold now! Would it be catalogued as "Believed to be the first copy to be offered at public sale as no copy is recorded in American Book-Prices Current from 1916 to date?" I believe it would. And why? Well, simply because the Brinley sale took place before 1916 and it is only since 1916 that Indexes have been compiled for American Book-Prices Current. Some of the auction houses believe, apparently, that a rare book's auction record is worth investigating if the trouble of looking it up is confined to searching three volumes of Indexes (1916-1922; 1923-1932; 1933-1940). Before 1916 the volumes might as well not have been issued as far as they are concerned.

There is, of course, a compilation in four volumes, edited by Luther S. Livingston, entitled Auction Prices of Books: Covering Representative Selections of Books from English Book Prices Current in 1886, and American Book Prices Current from 1894 to 1904 (New York, 1905), which many of us find useful. A glance at it would have dispelled (among other illusions) the "belief" that the Clemens copy of Byron's Fare Thee Well! was "the first appearance at public sale."

But it is frivolous, I suppose, to ask accuracy over a period of years when it is not achieved over a period of months. For example, in the Meyer sale, an eight-page folio, Indian Treaty, was given a full-page illustration and catalogued under "Washington,

George," with the note: "An apparently unrecorded issue of this important Indian Treaty. Research has located no other copy or reference to any copy of it."[32] Six months later, in the McHenry sale by the same gallery, there appeared a different copy of the same treaty, catalogued under "Indian Treaty" (also given a full-page illustration), with the note: "Apparently no copy of this treaty is recorded as having appeared at Public Sale."[33]

Again, in "believed to be's" and "apparently's" consider the Littell copy of Figueroa's *Manifesto* (Monterey, 1835). The description is headed: "Believed to be the only known Perfect Copy," and, again in the body of the note: "Apparently the only Perfect Copy."[34] There follows a census of known copies: "There are five copies known to us. . . ," and enumerated are the following: the copy in the Bancroft Library (lacking wrappers); one in the California State Library (lacking the 'Nota del Impresor and Erate') and the Dunlap copy (with the last leaf in facsimile). That accounts for three of the five. What of the other two? The catalogue note states: ". . . unfortunately we have no information on the Coronel and Lees copies." It was, I submit, an unwarranted assumption on the basis of their own census, for the Galleries to label the Littell copy as they did. There was an assumption without the slightest evidence that the two copies of which no knowledge was admitted were imperfect! This is not sound bibliographical thinking. Furthermore, this description was used in the Americana sale of H.C. Holmes, when this same copy was sold: the same description and the same census and the same statement: "There are five other known copies. . ."[35] Such reprinting of old descriptions when a book comes up for resale not only ignores the fact that physical deterioration in its condition may, quite possibly, have taken place, but takes no account of what subsequent research may have discovered.

The American Art Association used Robert E. Cowan's *A Bibliography of the Spanish Press of California* (printed in 1919) in listing the "five other known copies." Twenty-one years later, in reprinting this 1924 description practically verbatim, there was no effort made to check with George L. Harding's *A Census of California Spanish Imprints* (1933) which locates copies at Bancroft (3); California State Library; Coronel Collection, Los Angeles Museum; Templeton Crocker; J. Faunt-Leroy; Mrs. R.B. Henderson; Huntington; Mrs. K.C. Jamieson; The Old Mission,

Santa Barbara; and T.W. Streeter--no less than twelve, altogether.
Often (as we have just seen) reasonably fresh and up-to-date
bibliographical information is as ignored as are auction records
before 1916. It is an old stunt to catalogue a book by mentioning
where it cannot be found, rather than where it can, but it is not
considered the best bibliographical practice. Consider the recent
sale where a Bible with the Ephrate, 1787 imprint, is catalogued as
"excessively rare and not in O'Callaghan."[36] There is no mention
that it is in Evans, No. 20235. Nor is there any indication that
O'Callaghan's *List of Editions of Holy Scripture Printed in America
Prior to 1860*, was published in Albany as long ago as 1861. Or,
look at an item in the "New York Collector's" sale. It is described
with the note (in capitals): "This edition is not recorded by Evans
or Hildeburn."[37] Yet it is not mentioned that its whole story is in
Sabin, No. 5697.

Then there is the question of the general misuse of *S. T. C.*
entries, of which Donald Wing complained in his introduction to his
able continuation (New York, 1945). The "New York Collector's"
sale lists the third edition of Coke on Littleton, with the note: "not
listed in the Short-Title Catalogue."[38] It is listed there: No. 15786,
correctly entered under Littleton. The overlooking of this is an
error that any of us could make, however, in the haste of
cataloguing. But too many *S. T. C.* books have come to America
since the publication of that volume for any conscientious
cataloguer to make a virtue of the fact (without further research)
that it may list only one library here as possessing a copy of any
particular book. And this is especially true since the publication of
W.W. Bishop's most useful *A Checklist of American Copies of
S. T. C. Books* (University of Michigan, 1945). A single example
will suffice. In the Maclay sale the description of Peacham's *The
Complete Gentleman* (London, 1622) is headed: ". . . only one
copy recorded as being in America by the Short-Title Catalogue,"
and the note reads: "The Huntington copy is the only one reported
in America by the Short-Title Catalogue."[39] But that doesn't alter
the fact that Pforzheimer has a copy, as well as Yale, Folger,
Library of Congress, Newberry, Harvard, Williams and Columbia.

Our best attempt at a magazine for book collectors -- *The
Colophon* -- was the labor of love of a few people who hoped it
would prove a useful medium of exchange for bibliographical
knowledge. It had some remarkable articles in it. One hears

rumors of its revival -- may they be true! But, useful as it proved to collectors and others, most auction houses never, apparently, heard of it. At least they took little notice of it. In the conflicting descriptions of Pope's *The Dunciad*, referred to at the beginning of this article, R.H. Griffith's very able paper, *The Dunciad Duodecimo* in: *The Colophon* (Autumn, 1938) was completely ignored. William H. McCarthy, Jr. wrote for it an article (1936) disproving Wise's contention that the first issue of Byron's *The Corsair* ends on page 100, and has the printer's imprint -- furthermore he proves that "the true first issue of Byron's *The Corsair*, therefore, is a pamphlet of 108 pages without a printer's imprint on page 100."[40] Yet the Clemens copy was catalogued in 1945 with the heading: "The Rare First Issue" and described as "ending at page 100 . . . printer's imprint on the same leaf."[41]

F.W. Heron can present in the 1936 *Colophon* plain and concrete evidence that there are two separate printings of the title-page of the Appleton, 1866, *Alice*,[42] yet the description of the last American *Alice* sold at auction makes no reference to his findings.[43] George T. Goodspeed can do a beautiful bibliographical job in the same magazine in 1939 on the *First American 'Queen Mab,'*[44] documenting the whole story. He not only proved that the New York, J. Baldwin, 1821 imprint is not *bona fide* but showed where, when, why and by whom the book was produced, and established the true first American edition as New York, 1831. Yet we find the Newton copy of the 1831 edition catalogued as "Second American edition,"[45] and we find a copy of the New York, 1821 edition catalogued last year with reference to the Goodspeed article, as: "Apparently the first (unauthorized) edition,"[46] which is what it isn't.

The learned cataloguer of the renowned Pforzheimer library[47] there concludes (to give just one example) that of Ben Jonson's *Workes*, 1616: "the engraved title is known in three states. There is little evidence for assigning any particular order to them but the following seems probable. The variations all occur in the imprint.

[A] In what may be the earliest it reads: London | Printed by | W. | Stansby and are | to be sould by | Rich. Meighen | An° D 1616.

[B] In what appears to be a later state it reads: London | Printed by William | Stansby | An° D 1616.

[C] The third (?) state which is found in all recorded large-paper copies as well as in some small-paper, reads: Imprinted at | London by |Will Stansby. | An° D 1616 |"

Yet in the Gribbel sale, the 1616 edition of the *Workes* of Ben Jonson is catalogued with the categorical statement: "First issue with the imprint of 'Will Stansby.' In the second issue the name is spelled 'William Stansby' and in the third the name of R. Meighen is added."[48] Truly the first shall be last and the last shall be first. It is curious, incidentally, that several of our auction houses have never, to my knowledge, referred to this great Pforzheimer catalogue when dealing with books of the period. Let us hope that some attention will be paid to it when it comes time to catalogue the splendid third part of the late Frank J. Hogan's library--the Elizabethans![b]

William Merritt Sale's excellent *Bibliography of Samuel Richardson* (New Haven, 1936) points out several variants in *Clarissa* (1748) and *Sir Charles Grandison* (1754), yet these titles were recently catalogued[49] without any reference to his findings.

John Carter can point out (as long ago as 1936) the highly important fact that the second edition of Mrs. Browning's *Poems* in two volumes (London, Chapman and Hall, 1850) -- a book of considerable interest for it contains, among other new matter, the first printing of *Sonnets from the Portuguese*, and as such now takes its place in the "Grolier Hundred" -- is found with two different title-pages and three different bindings.[50] Yet not once has any reference to his findings been made and, as a result, not one of the ten copies sold by American auction houses since its disvovery has been correctly described.

Harris F. Fletcher's monumental work on Milton[51] cannot have caught the eye of auction houses, else the Pershing copy of Milton's *Poems* (London, 1673) would scarcely have been catalogued as "Lacks portrait,"[52] when Fletcher shows it is practically certain that it was never issued with one, while at the same time the important matter of the variant imprints is not even mentioned.

It is discouraging, also, to note that when a really distinguished collection of Goethe[53] appears at auction sale in America (to be sold January 21-22, 1946) it is catalogued without the slightest reference to the magnificent Yale University catalogue of the *Speck Collection of Goetheana: Goethe's Works with the*

Exception of Faust (New Haven, 1940). Its use would have answered all of the queries on signatures and would have avoided designating an octavo as a duodecimo, which occurs some twenty-five times.

But then too, its use would have avoided the following most unusual and wholly delightful (and completely erroneous) description of Goethe's *West-oestlicher Divan* (Stuttgart, 1819):[54] "Most . . . copies have the pages 7-10 cut out, which were replaced by a piece of *cardboard*." (!) The Yale catalogue, in describing its copies, states: "First edition, pp. 7-10 are in both the cancelled (Sig. I_{4-5}) and the canceling (Sig. 35_{3-5}) form . . . . Variant: the cancelled form of pp. 7-10 is missing, and the canceling form has been inserted in its place." The French and Germans have a single word for this -- *carton*. One must pursue this word far enough in a good dictionary to get beyond "cardboard," to discover that it also means "cancel." The use of the Yale catalogue would also have prevented other errors.

In the *Southwest Review* and later in her *Letters of Wise to Wrenn*,[55] Miss Fannie E. Ratchford pointed out the fact that Tennyson's so-called *Idylls of the Hearth* "is a fraud -- a mere first edition of *Enoch Arden* with a forged title-page." Yet the Pershing copy of *Idylls of the Hearth* was catalogued as "First Edition. One of a small number issued before the title-page was changed to Enoch Arden, etc. . . ."[56] And Ronald Baughman's[57] researches in regard to Matthew Arnold's *Alaric at Rome* made it clear that when the type-fascimile reprint was made in 1893 from the first discovered copy of this rare piece, under Wise's supervision and editorship, a number of extra copies were stuck off without the prefatory matter and passed off as originals. Two copies of *Alaric at Rome* came up at auction last year[58] and in the description of neither of them were Mr. Baughman's findings mentioned.

But lest we think ourselves a trifle better regarded than *The Colophon*, the Pforzheimer library catalogue, the auction houses' own catalogues, most recent bibliographies, etc., may I point out that the auction houses pay no more attention to the *Papers of the Bibliographical Society of America*. I know of no reason to assume they will make an exception of the present case. John Alden can point out the fact that the Mein (Boston) edition of the *Vicar* was, like that of the *Sentimental Journey*, the earliest to appear in America: "Published in 1767, it antedates the 1772

Philadelphia edition which has commonly been considered the first. As such, a copy of the Philadelphia edition was offered for sale in the recent auction of the library of A. Edward Newton,"[59] But the Philadelphia editions of both the *Vicar* and *Sentimental Journey* are still being offered as "First American Editions."[60] And this is from no dislike of Boston, for Marshall W.S. Swan, in discussing the bibliographical problems of the Boston editions of Shakespeare's *Poems*,[61] demonstrates that the 1807 Boston editions were preceded by the Philadelphia edition of 1796 but the auction houses still catalogue Boston, 1807 as "first American edition."[62] Frank Willson in *That 'Gilded Age' Again: An Attempt to Unmuddle the Mystery of the Fifty-seven Variants*,[63] thoroughly demolished the accuracy of the old standard description of "First Issue with the rate 1873 title-page and without the illustration called for at page 403," but no attention is paid to him.[64]

Again, in 1942, Paul Angle[65] disclosed to the Society the vastly important fact that the Baker & Godwin, New York, 1863 edition was not the first appearance in print (aside from newspaper publication) of Lincoln's *Gettysburg Address*, yet the only copy sold at auction since then ignored his findings.[66]

It will be instructive to see how long it will be before Philo Calhoun's and Howell Heaney's recent excellent study of Dickens' *A Christmas Carol*[67] will be consulted.

When, occasionally, fresh bibliographical information is mentioned, it is not always used consistently, nor in some cases accurately. For example, in the notes to the Hogan copy of *Lyrical Ballads* (Bristol, 1798) it is conceded that leaf G (pp. 97-98) exists in only one state, quoting such authorities as Whicher in *The Colophon*, New Series, Vol. 2, p. 370; Partington in *Forging Ahead* (New York, 1939), p. 39; and Edwin Wells in *The Times Literary Supplement*, January 17, 1942, admitting that "the supposed cancel leaf noted by Dr. Wise has been accepted as a forgery."[68] Yet all this is forgotten in the cataloguing by the same gallery of the more recent Pershing copy of the London issue, where the statement (previously discredited in the Hogan description) is flatly made: "First state of this issue with the leaf G (p. 97-98) in the First State . . . in the cancelled leaf this was changed,"[69] etc. Again, in cataloguing the Pershing copy of *The Faerie Queene* (London, 1590), Francis R. Johnson's plain statement of fact is distorted. The Pershing copy is noted as having, among other things: "the sonnets at the end in both states, occupying leaves Pp-Pp_8 and the four unpaged leaves Qq-Qq_4 . . . the variations among copies in these respects are no longer considered indications of earlier or later issues. Cf. Francis R. Johnson's *A Critical Bibliography of the Works of Edmund Spenser.* . . (Baltimore, 1933), pp. 11-18."[70] Now here are Johnson's conclusions as to the bibliographical status of *The Faerie Queen* 1590) as I read them. He explicitly maintains, in the pages quoted, that, as to these sonnets, we do have a legitimate differentiation. He says (p. 15): "There are two issues of these sonnets printed . . . It is only with reference to these sonnets that we have any sound basis for distinguishing two issues of the first edition of the *Faerie Queene*.", and "Copies containing the first issue only end with [Pp_8]."

Finally, there should be, I think, much closer liaison between auction houses and the compilers of *American Book-Prices Current*. The editor of that useful work gets a catalogue from an auction house and later a list of prices at which the various items sold. He does not get, I am informed, and has no way of finding out, what books or manuscripts are occasionally returned after a sale for any of a variety of reasons. As a result these "wrong" items become duly canonized in *American Book-Prices Current* and are thus given an air of false respectability. It would be most useful if a list of "returns" were supplied to the editor so that these items might be eliminated from the yearly volumes.

As it is now, it is only when an item which has been returned is eventually re-catalogued with a correct description, that it becomes a matter of record. For example, in Part 3 of the Gribbel sale, an autograph manuscript of Jonathan Swift appeared.[71] After the sale it was returned and made another appearance in Sale 707 as "a contemporary manuscript in an unknown hand,"[72] with the complete story.

Here the record is clear for all to read. But, to give just one example, what about the Hogan copy of Holmes' *The Autocrat of the Breakfast Table* in the so-called five-star binding?[73] Following the sale this was returned as defective. It is of slight concern that this is entered in *American Book-Prices Current* from the point of view of price, but its entry from the viewpoint of a census of known copies in this rare binding is another matter. In cataloguing this item the galleries, of course, completely neglected Currier's article and census in the *Papers of the Bibliographical Society of*

America.[74] And it was entirely fortuitous, and not due to information supplied by the galleries, that Andre's *The Chow Chace* is entered in *American Book-Prices Current* correctly as a "contemporary transcript" and not as an "Autograph Manuscript, signed," as it was catalogued in the Drexel sale.[75]

As evidence of the fact that it is not completely unknown for corrections to be made in *American Book-Prices Current* even after the yearly volume has been printed, there is Button Gwinnett's *Bible*, the Spencer-Parker-Diard copy, sold on March 9, 1926, entered in *American Book-Prices Current* for that year (p. 53), price $10,000. Over this entry in all copies are three red rules, above which are the words in red, "no sale." Incidentally, when this book made its reappearance in Part 4 of the Gribbel sale its previous auction record was not mentioned.[76] Colton Storm saw fit to enter this in the 1945 *American Book-Prices Current* with a reference to its 1926 record.

I would like to make clear, finally, that this plea for a more consistent policy of cataloguing by auction houses is addressed to all American Auction galleries handling books. The record of all of them leaves something to be desired, in my opinion, and the sales of one of them have been drawn upon as examples more frequently than others merely because, through its pre-eminence in its field, it has therefore handled a much larger volume of American and English literature, with which I am chiefly concerned in this paper.

A very large volume of books handled by auction in America is correctly and properly described, though, I may add, there is very little that requires more than a simple physical description of perhaps ninety percent of them. I know perfectly well, from sad and sometimes bitter experience, that complete accuracy in bibliographical descriptions is unobtainable by any cataloguer, bibliographer, dealer or even librarian, for that matter. But I feel most strongly that the more attention to standardizing nomenclature, fewer inconsistencies in cataloguing, less use of pretentious claims which even moderate research demolishes, less verbatim reprinting of old descriptions, a closer relationship with the compiler of *American Book-Prices Current*, and a much greater use of the tools constantly produced by modern bibliographical research is certainly desired.

NOTES

[a]An answer to the 28 July article, signed "Parke-Bernet Galleries, Inc.," was printed in the same newspaper on 2 March 1946.--Editor.

[1]Library formed by the late Dr. James B. Clemens. January 8-9, 1945. Parke-Bernet Galleries. Item 361.

[2]The Frank J. Hogan Library. Part Two. English Literature Mainly of the XVIII and XIX Centuries. April 24-25, 1945. Parke-Bernet Galleries. Item 561.

[3]Rare English and French Literature . . . Collected by the late Bronson Winthrop. March 12-13, 1945. Parke-Bernet Galleries. Item 644.

[4]Hogan. Part Two. *Op. cit.* Items 562-563.

[5]Selections from the Library of a New York Collector. October 15-16, 1945. Parke-Bernet Galleries. Item 94.

[6]*Op. cit.* Item 90.

[7]Rare Books . . . Collected by the late A. Edward Newton. April 16-18, 1941. Parke-Bernet Galleries. Item 403.

[8]Hogan. Part Two. *Op. cit.* Item 183.

[9]French Literature, etc. November 6 and 8, 1945. Parke-Bernet Galleries. Item 366.

[10]*Op. cit.* Item 278.

[11]Rare books from the libraries of George M. LaMonte and Leonard Outhwaite. March 5, 1940. G.A. Barker & Co. Item 17.

[12]The Frank J. Hogan Library. Part One. American Authors. January 23-24, 1945. Parke-Bernet Galleries. Item 89.

[13]Hogan. Part One. *Op. cit.* Item 86.

[14]Rare and Valuable Books (Various Owners). June 8-9, 1944. Samuel T. Freeman & Co. Item 199.

[15]*Op. cit.* Items 13-14.

[16]*Op. cit.* Item 194.

[17](Various Owners.) June 17, 1944. Parke-Bernet Galleries. Item 178.

[18]Hogan. Part One. *Op. cit.* Item 192.

[19]*Op. cit.* Item 279.

[20]Hogan. Part One. *Op. cit.* Item 578

[21]Hogan. Part One. *Op. cit.* Item 391.

[22]New York Collector. *Op. cit.* Item 287.

[23]*Op. cit.* Item 418.

[24]*Op. cit.* Item 419.

[25]*Op. cit.* Item 126.

[26](Various Owners.) December 10-11, 1945. Parke-Bernet Galleries. Item 94.

[27](Various Owners.) April 28, 1944. Wm. D. Morley, Inc. Item 66.

[28]The renowned library of the late John A. Spoor. Part One. April 26-28, 1939. Parke-Bernet Galleries. Item 124.

[29]The library of the late Ogden Goelet. Part Two. January 24-25, 1935. American Art Association. Item 51.

[30]Library of Judge Jacob Klein. Part One. February 9-10, 1911. Anderson Auction Co. Item 229.

[31]Library of Charles C. Johnston. . . . October 4, 22-23, 1912. Anderson Auction Co. Item 169.

[32]Historical and Literary Autographs, etc., collected by the late Alfred C. Meyer. Second Part. November 30, December 1, 1943. Parke-Bernet Galleries. Item 320.

[33]The James McHenry Papers. Part One. May 3, 1944. Parke-Bernet Galleries. Item 87.

[34]The Distinguished Collection of Americana formed by C.G. Littell. February 5-6, 1945. Parke-Bernet Galleries. Item 348.

[35]Americanana . . . . Property of Mr. H.C. Holmes. January 7-9, 1924. American Art Association. Item 397.

[36](Various Owners. Sale Number 696.) October 22-23, 1945. Parke-Bernet Galleries. Item 59.

[37]*Op. cit.* Item 77.

[38]*Op. cit.* Item 172.

[39]Five Centuries of Sport . . . . Formed by the late Alfred B. Maclay. April 10-11, 1945. Parke-Bernet Galleries. Item 462.

[40]*The First Edition of Byron's 'Corsair'* in *The Colophon*, New Series, Vol. II, Number 1 (Autumn, 1936).

[41]*Op. cit.* Item 115.

[42]*Op. cit.* New Series, Vol. I. Number 3. (Winter, 1936.)

[43]Hogan. Part Two. *Op. cit.* Item 157.

[44]*Op. cit.* New Graphic Series. Number 1.

[45]*Op. cit.* Item 253.

[46](Various Owners. Sale Number 643.) March 5-6, 1945. Parke-Bernet Galleries. Item 588.

[47]The Carl H. Pforzheimer Library. English Literature 1475-1700. (New York, Privately Printed, 1940.) 3 volumes. Item 559.

[48]Autograph Letters, Manuscripts and Rare Books collected by the late John Gribbel. Part Four (May 7-8, 1945.) Parke-Bernet Galleries. Item 292.

[b]The sale catalogue of the third part of the Frank J. Hogan library, Parke-Bernet Galleries, April 22-24, 1946, made copious use of the Pforzheimer Catalogue.--Editor.

[49]City Book Auction Sale. Number 322. November 3, 1945. Items 289-290.

[50]*The* [London] *Times Literary Supplement* (May 30, 1936).

[51]John Milton's Complete Poetical Works Reproduced in Photograph Fascimile. . . . Vol. I. (The University of Illinois Press, 1943.)

[52]The Distinguished Library of James H. Pershing. November 26-27, 1945. Parke-Bernet Galleries. Item 209.

[53]Standard Sets . . . German Classic Literature . . . Collected by the late C.W. Chappell. January 21-22, 1946. Parke-Bernet Galleries.

[54]*Op. cit.* Item 206.

[55]New York, Knopf, 1944.

[56]*Op. cit.* Item 300.

[57]*Huntington Library Bulletin.* Number 9. (April, 1936)

[58]Hogan. Part Two. *Op. cit.* Item 1. Clemens. *Op. cit.* Item 57.

[59]"John Mein . . . Detection" in: Bibliographical Society of America, *Papers*, Vol. XXXVI (Third Quarter, 1942).

[60]Hogan. Part Two. *Op. cit.* Items 332 and 682.

[61]"Shakespeare's 'Poems.' The First Three Boston Editions,"in Bibliographical Society of America, *Papers*, Vol. XXXVI (First Quarter, 1942).

[62]Pershing. *Op. cit.* Item 264.

[63]Bibliographical Society of America, *Papers*, Vol. XXXVII (Second Quarter, 1943).

[64](Various Owners.) Sale Number 107. January 25, 1945. Swann Auction Galleries. Item 268.

[65]"Four Lincoln Firsts" in: Bibliographical Society of America, *Papers*, Vol. XXXVI (First Quarter, 1942).

[66]Lincolniana. Sale Number 121. June 7, 1945. Swann Auction Galleries. Item 245.

[67]"Dickens' 'Christmas Carol' After a Hundred Years: A Study in Bibliographical Evidence, in: Bibliographical Society of America, *Papers*, Vol. XXXIX (Fourth Quarter, 1945).

[68]Hogan. Part Two. *Op. cit.* Item 795.

[69]*Op. cit.* Item 350.

[70]*Op. cit.* Item 282.

[71]Autograph Letters, Manuscripts and Rare Books Collected by the late John Gribbel. Part Three. April 16-17, 1945. Parke-Bernet Galleries. Item 345.

[72](Various Owners. Sale 707, misnumbered 711.) November 19-20, 1945. Parke-Bernet Galleries. Item 515.

[73]Hogan. Part One. *Op. cit.* Item 285.

[74]Vol. XXXVIII, No. 3, 1944.

[75]Literary and Historical Autograph Manuscripts. . . . Property of the Drexel Institute of Technology. October 17-18, 1944. Parke-Bernet Galleries. Item 7.

[76]*Op. cit.* Item 225.

12
IPEX (1963)

This is a review of the exhibition known as "Printing and the Mind of Man" held in London in the summer and autumn of 1963. The Lilly Library was major contributor to the exhibition, lending thirty-one items, over half of the total sent from America. In 1964 the Lilly Library held its own "Printing and the Mind of Man' exhibition with 188 of the 412 original titles, and on the tenth anniversary of the London show the Lilly Library was able to mount an exhibition that contained 75 percent of the titles in the 1963 catalogue. [From Antiquarian Bookman, 32 (September 30, 1963): 1199-1201.]

The Eleventh International Printing Machinery and Allied Trades Exhibition (IPEX), held recently in London, was the largest and most comprehensive of its kind ever assembled. Two exhibitions of books were held under the general title "Printing and the Mind of Man." The larger one, on Influential Books, so to speak, was held at Earls Court for only two weeks, July 16-27. A smaller one, of Fine Printing, continued in the King's Library of the British Museum, through September. The former was a loan exhibition; the latter almost entirely drawn from the Museum's own resources. These notes are concerned with the Earls Court exhibition only.

Flanking the entrance to the first room of the exhibition were two prefatory panels. The first was a greatly enlarged print of the first page of the Gutenberg Bible with a pencil spotlight picking out the words *Fiat Lux*. The caption read:

"Here are the first words of all the thousands of printed books that have been illuminating the mind of man through these five centuries.

"With the sacred words *Fiat Lux--Let there be light*--printing foretold its momentous destiny.

"This exhibition tells the story of the invention that broadened and extended the light of scripture; the light of ancient wisdom; the light of modern knowledge; the dawn light of scientific thought.

"Printing, that was to rescue the common man from the darkness of illiteracy, was born repeating the words *Fiat Lux.*"

The other panel read:

"Here you will see the primitive tools that brought about a vast revolution in human thinking, as the printing press and movable type opened new windows to knowledge in Philosophy and Religion, Science and Invention, Political Ideas and Social Theory.

"Here you may see how mechanical invention rose to the demands of the ever-widening literate public and turned the handicraft of Gutenberg into the colossal industry which IPEX displays.

"Here you will find the original editions of books that have changed and expanded man's vision of himself and of his world through these five centuries."

Between these panels was a case displaying a unique leaf of the Gutenberg Bible, "thought by some other incunabulists to be a sheet (with only one of its four pages printed) discarded at the press. In either case it is the only example of its kind known to exist." This description of the very first lot in the catalogue contains, as seems so very often the case, an error. Two of the four pages, not one, are printed.

Displayed with this was the unique Caxton *Letter of Indulgence*, dated 13 December 1476. The catalogue notes that "this is the first known piece of printing in England; and it is probable that the last will be a piece of jobbing work too, since Armageddon is more prone to proclamations than to sonnet sequences."

The first room was devoted to typefounding and printing, with a working typefoundry, displaying punches of the sixteenth to twentieth centuries, matrices of the same periods, a caster's furnace, type moulds, typefounder's specimens and the like in profusion. There was also a reconstructed early printing house, a display devoted to printing ink, etc. This "retrospective survey of technical processes" was assembled under the direction of Mr. Charles Batey, Printer Emeritus to the University of Oxford.

From this room one entered the main display space, devoted to the printed books, and historic printing machinery. The first case contained that famous masterpiece of printing, the Latin *Psalter*, John Fust and Peter Schoeffer, Mainz, 14 August 1457, on vellum the Queen's copy from the Royal Library at Windsor. Flanking this was a panel: *The Impact of Printing*:

"This attempt to illustrate the impact of the printed word on the human mind is the most impressive collection of books of this kind ever gathered under one roof.

"Lack of space and human fallibility have caused omissions that are lamentable and inclusions that may be questionable.

"Nevertheless we are proud of our achievement and we invite you with confidence to a feast of learning. It is a gargantuan meal and although the robust appetite may digest it in one huge swallow it is best taken in small portions at frequent intervals."

That this was "the most impressive collection of books ever gathered under one roof" was no idle boast. An immense amount of work and impressive collaboration went into assembling it, sixty-three individuals and libraries lending books.

Consider those sent from the United States alone. Ten private owners and seven public institutions lent more than sixty books, over 10 percent of those on display.

Individual owners were most generous in allowing their treasures to make the double voyage. Among the great rarities lent were the unique proof sheets of the London, 1865, *Alice* (Alfred Berol); the first separate printing of *The Gettysburg Solemnities*, Washington, 1863, one of three recorded, (Carl Haverlin); *Pilgrim's Progress*, London, 1678, so fine a copy that it was not opened, the binding being shown with a photostat title page, (William H. Schiede); the *Communist Manifesto*, London, 1848, a mint copy in original printed wrappers, (Charles J. Rosenbloom); Montaigne's *Essaies*, Bordeaux, 1580, in original binding, (Louis H. Silver); Pigafetta's *Voyage*, Paris, 1525, (Thomas Streeter); and fourteen books from Bern Dibner, ranging from William Gilbert, 1600, to Max Planck, 1900.

Indiana's Lilly Library lent over half the works from America including its unique Gutenberg leaf, mentioned above; the first broadside issue of *The Declaration of Independence*, (Philadelphia, 1776); the first Latin Columbus *Letter*, (Rome, 1493, "Harrisse no. 1"); the "Eliot Indian Bible", (Cambridge, 1663-1), on through Sir Alexander Fleming's *Penicillium*, (London, 1929).

An impressive display of books came from British libraries, naturally, also from French, Dutch, German, Italian, Swiss, Swedish, Danish, private and public sources, among others.

It came as a surprise to those who did not know of his interests, (though for years he has listed under his "Recreations" in *Who's Who*, "First Edition Collecting") that Ian Fleming was by long odds the largest individual loaner to the exhibit, with forty-four books. Amusingly, one of these was the only recorded copy in original parts of Baden-Powell's *Scouting for Boys*, (London, 1908). Surely this was not one of the books James Bond devoured as a youth. No Boy Scout he!

The gathering of so many rarities from so many varied sources was no overnight achievement--it represented, as a matter of fact, 18 months of work.

A very few books could not be obtained in their original editions. The Pierpont Morgan copy of Caxton's first printing of *The Canterbury Tales* among them; but then they wouldn't lend this to the Lilly Grolier show either. They did, however, contribute other books. The *Book of Common Prayer* was represented by the 6 June issue, rather than that of 7 March, which would have been available for the asking. The Boston Public Libraries copy, one of the only four in America, was on exhibition at the time at the Lilly Library's Grolier show.

The fact that certain books were lent from America or the continent, does not necessarily mean that no copies were available in England. It was simply easier, in some cases, as a matter of logistics, to borrow a number of books from a single source. The British Museum, at this time, lends no books, though we understand this restriction is to be lifted shortly.

It is interesting to note that most of the books which were not available in their original editions are comparatively modern. Lobatchewsky's *Geometry*, (St. Petersburg 1829), could not be secured, though the Russian government lent a copy to the Grolier Club for their noted science exhibition (And when, by the way, is that catalogue to appear?). Pavlov's *Verdauungsdrüsen* was represented by the first German, (Wiesbaden, 1898), and not its original Russian edition. A unique copy of Louis Braille's original book on printing for the blind (Paris, 1829), is known but could not be lent because of its extreme fragility. And so recent a work as

Fleming's *Penicillium* had to be represented by a 1940 reprint of the original 1929 offprint.

A few books arrived too late to be included in the printed catalogue. The Italian edition of Marco Polo is listed there (Venice, 1496), though the actual first German edition (Nuremberg, 1477) was shown. The edition of Erasmus' *Colloquies* exhibited was Basel, 1516, not 1524, and Lewis and Clark's *Expedition*, was represented by the London, 1814 edition, not the Philadelphia.

The catalogue itself makes no pretense to bibliographical niceties in its descriptions. Issues or states are seldom mentioned. Paine's *Rights of Man* (London, 1791) and the *Communist Manifesto* (London, 1848), are both first issues, though unidentified as such. Bindings, even when original and important, (as on the Eliot *Bible*) are seldom stressed. Association interest is very occasionally mentioned, though of John Smith's *General History*, (London, 1624), it was allowed to be recorded that the copy on exhibition is "the dedication copy to Frances, Duchess of Richard and Lennox."

What is properly stressed are the reasons why the books are included in the exhibition. The descriptions are in many cases marvels of condensation--occasionally under seventy-five words. And generally they go to the heart of the matter. A typical example is Frederick Winslow Taylor's *The Principles of Scientific Management*, (New York, 1911--and how often do you find that in rare book dealers' catalogues?):

"F.W. Taylor, and American engineer employed by the Bethlehem Steel Company, was the founder of 'scientific management' in industry. He laid down the main lines of approach to the problem of increased efficiency by standardizing processes and machines, time and motion study, and systematizing 'piecework' or payment by results. All these systems have been welcomed in Russia, but are anathema to trade unionists almost everywhere else."

And F.J. Turner's *The Significance of the Frontier*, (Wisconsin, 1894):

"One of those *simplificateurs terrible*. Turner tried to explain the whole of American history as an urge to push forward 'the frontier'. Rejected by historians, the term has become an integral part of American folklore and journalistic mythology. Its latest issue is the slogan of the 'new frontier' adopted by the Kennedy administration."

There will be a great scurrying among dealers' stocks (and for the matter of that, librarians' card catalogues), when this list comes to general attention.

The inclusions underline the fact that all rare books are not important, nor are all important books rare, nor are all influential books universally recognized as such. The guiding hands of Percy Muir, of Elkin Mathews, Ltd., that imaginative firm of rare book dealers, and of John Carter, ever a pioneer of "New Paths in Bookcollecting," both on various of the committees, are everywhere evident in this main section of the exhibition. The Exhibition of Fine Printing was under the direction of Sir Frank Francis, Director and Principal Librarian of the British Museum.

Inevitably there will be wails of anguish about the inclusions or exclusions. Why include Walpole's *Castle of Otranto*, London, 1765, (lent by Wilmarth Lewis) on the grounds that it influenced the dead Gothic novel, and exclude Poe's *Murders in the Rue Morgue*, Philadelphia, 1843, which so vitally guided the still flourishing detective story? And why Robert G. Ingersoll, of all people, and no Upton Sinclair? And so on. This questioning and prodding is all to the good. Let's have someone make up a list of books they feel should have been included, and weren't.

There was criticism that creative poetry (with few exceptions) was excluded. This, the Committee says, was because it elevated the *spirit* of man and they were concerned with the *mind* of man. And, anyway, for England at least, there is always John Hayward's notable catalogue and why try to duplicate what had been so well done already. And there was, after all, the available space to be considered. All fair enough, but it might have been better to have originally excluded all poetry (and fiction as well). But these are minor considerations and no selective exhibition ever pleases everyone and generally those who put it on the least of all. They know the compromises which have had to be made.

The exhibition was housed in handsome show cases, especially designed for the occasion by John Lansdell, and built at a cost of £ 9,000. They were generously given, after the exhibition, to the British Museum.

A small room leading off the main hall held an exhibition of Illustrations stressing prephotographic processes. This contained woodcuts, copperplates, variants of line-etching, lithography, examples of compositions without type, photo composition, filmsetting, etc.

The exit door led into the modern wonderland of awesome machinery which formed the rest of the exhibition, a 450-page catalogue of which is available for 5/. A panel at the exit read:

"Your journey through five centuries has brought to this threshold. Now as you make your way out into the modern wonderland of IPEX 1963, you come back to a world in which the spoken word as well as the written, can be infinitely multiplied.

"But printing will stand alone through the centuries to come as the Gateway to The Freedoms of the Literate Mind; the freedom to stop and ponder without losing the thread; the freedom to turn back and challenge any glib assumption at the start; the freedom to turn to the end and see whatever subtle intention it may reveal.

"In this century printing has swept the light of literacy across whole new nations, beckoning new millions to responsible citizenship. Before the year 2000 the entire human race will be reaching for the priceless gifts that printing brought to the mind of man."

The exhibition itself was well attended during its too-brief life. By almost everyone but the trade, that is. Numbers of the younger and alert dealers came, not once, but many times. It was a little astonishing, to this observer at least, to have too many senior members of the trade remark after it closed that it was a good show, *they were told*. Somehow, they hadn't found time to see it.

The reception accorded it by the British press was also incomprehensible. They did nothing to promote it, or exploit it, or do anything much about it. *The Times Literary Supplement* ran two articles, largely about the esthetics of printing, which had nothing to do with the show at all. Like the croaking of Poe's *Raven*, they "little meaning, little relevancy bore", to the matter at hand. Not a single word was said of the superb catalogue, available at the give-away price of 10/6--and sold at the exhibition itself for 5/. If, as Shaw remarked, the British don't deserve great men, even less do they deserve great exhibitions, at least of books. It was a heartening thing to have a voice from America trumpet to their shores clarion news of what they had ignored (AB--"The Best Book Buy of the Century", July 29, '63). Though the exhibition was shortlived, its influence, exerted through the catalogues, will long continue.

Questions of space, I have been told, limited some descriptions, illustrations, etc. There is talk of an expanded, more fully annotated and illustrated issue. We hope this is so but, even if it is not, all bookmen will remain indebted to the far-sighted souls who so ably conceived and produced "Printing and the Mind of Man."

13

GROLIER: OR 'TIS SIXTY YEARS SINCE (1963)

In his Preface to the catalogue for an exhibition mounted to celebrate a visit to The Lilly Library by members of the Grolier Club, Mr. Randall reflected upon the once popular practice of collecting books according to lists. [From Grolier: or 'Tis Sixty Years Since, A Reconstruction of the Exhibit of 100 Books Famous in English Literature Originally held in New York, 1903 on the Occasion of the Club's Visit to the Lilly Library, Indiana University May 1, 1963. Bloomington: Indiana University, The Lilly Library, 1963, pp. 3-5.]

THE first influential list of "One Hundred Books" was compiled by Sir John Lubbock (later Right Hon. Lord Avebury, P.C.) as Chapter IV, "The Choice of Books," in his charming series of essays, *The Pleasures of Life* (London, 1887). Quoting from the 1921 edition, Sir John wrote:

> Our ancestors had great difficulty in procuring books. Ours now is what to select. We must be careful what we read, and not, like the sailors of Ulysses, take bags of wind for sacks of treasure. . . . lest, as too often happens, we should waste time over trash . . . .
>
> I have often wished some one would recommend a list of a hundred good books. If we had such lists drawn up by a few good guides they would be useful. . . .
>
> In the absence of such lists I have picked out the books most frequently mentioned with approval by those who have referred directly or indirectly to the pleasure of reading, and have ventured to include some

which, through less frequently mentioned, are especial favourites of my own. . . .

I have abstained, for obvious reasons, from mentioning works by living authors . . . and I have omitted works on science, with one or two exceptions, because the subject is so progressive.

Sir John's famous list, which was first delivered as a lecture to the London Working Men's College, started a trend. Contemporary interest was so great that the London *Pall Mall Gazette* issued as "Extra" No. 24, "The Best Hundred Books by the Best Judges." Contributors included Lord Bryce, John Ruskin, and Wilkie Collins. Soon other "Hundred" lists were compiled by Lord Acton and Mr. Shorter. Sir John was not impressed. In the Preface to his latest edition available to me (London, 1921, "41st Edition--273rd Thousand"), he states: "Neither Lord Acton nor Mr. Shorter has convinced me that I should drop any of the books from my list." Mr. Shorter's list is condemned because "it is too light, too merely amusing . . . . He prefers *Rasselas* to Molière and finds a place for Rousseau's *Confessions*, Boccaccio, and *Tom Jones*."

Admitting Lord Acton's list does not suffer from levity, he complains that, though "of sterling worth, some [inclusions] seem to me too technical, some too special."

Modern taste would seem to agree with this, considering that Lord Acton includes Mignet's *Negociations Relatives a la Succession d'Espagna*, Carte's *Histoire du Mouvement Religieux dans le Canton de Vaud*, Schneckenburger's *Vergleichende Darstellung*, Hundeshagen's *Kirchenverfassungsgeschichte*, and similar reading. I had imagined until recently that it was from reading of this nature that Acton drew his famous statement: "Power corrupts and absolute power corrupts absolutely." But that was an earlier Acton.

Still, there is on Sir John's list at least one work, St. Hilaire's *Le Bouddha et sa religion*, which is not in one library I know of which has over a million and a half volumes, in *any* edition. Sir John's list is overloaded with Orientalia, and who today reads Samuel Smiles? Also, he fudged a little in his hundred on the works of Scott "which indeed, constitute a library in themselves, but which I must ask, in return for my trouble, to be allowed, as a special favour, to count as one."

He was a man of strong convictions. He lists Smith's *Wealth of Nations*, "part of"; Plato *Dialogues*, "at any rate, the Apology, Crito, and Phaedo," and adds that, though he includes the *Sheking* and the *Analects* of Confucius for their influence. "I must humbly confess I do not greatly admire either . . . . I may add that both works are quite short."

So far as I know, he made only two changes in his original list. In 1890 he added Kalidasa's *Sakuntala* and Schiller's *William Tell*, "omitting, in consequence, Lucretius and Miss Austen: Lucretius because, though his work is most remarkable, it is perhaps too difficult and therefore less generally suitable than most of the others on the list; and Miss Austen because English novelists were somewhat overrepresented." Ten were included.

List-makers of the "Best," "Good," "Influential," etc. still continue, one of the latest being by Somerset Maugham, and their compilers include such figures as Arnold Bennett and Sir Winston Churchill.

These lists were aimed, primarily, at self-education; remember Eliot's "Harvard Five Foot Shelf" (fifteen minutes reading a day equals a college education)? His list, by the way, admitted but one novel, Alessandro Manzonis' *I promessi sposi*, (Milan, 1825). The Grolier exhibition of *One Hundred Books Famous in English Literature* (New York, 1903), was not of this ilk. Nor was it intended to be a guide to collectors in the sense that A. Edward Newton's *One Hundred Good Novels* certainly was. A private exhibition, put on purely for the pleasure of the members, it was not planned as a collector's *Vade Mecum*.

Its influence, however, was considerable; whether for good or evil is moot and will not be argued here. To the degree that it stereotyped collecting habits, it was bad. But it was also a catalyst, stimulating many who might not else have collected at all, or at least as ardently. Mr. Lilly was one of these, though his interests rapidly widened. He acquired ninety-four per cent of the Grolier Hundred, ninety-nine per cent of Newton's. He is also the only collector I know of to have the temerity to tackle that distillation of all lists-- Asa Don Dickinson's *One Thousand Best Books*. Acquiring them in first editions, in their original languages, he was within sighting distance of ninety per cent completion when he retired from "this book-collecting game."

It seems unlikely that the members viewing the original exhibit on the Club's premises, then at 29 East 32nd Street, could possibly conceive of its reconstruction here, six decades later and nine hundred miles west. Nor could they have imagined the Club's migrating to Cincinnati, Ohio; Lexington, Kentucky; Bloomington, Indiana; and Ann Arbor, Michigan, to visit rare book libraries. There were, at that time, very few books west of the Hudson worth their getting their feet wet to examine.

Yet, as John T. Winterich says in his *Informal History* of the Club: "The Founders were men alike of vision and of affairs, they had some conception of the potentialities of their city and, very likely, of their Club." He also notes (how truly), "Bookmen long to go on pilgrimages, provided there are suitable shrines."

The present exhibition, based, of course, on J. K. Lilly's ninety-four per cent completion of the "100," has been generously fleshed out by the loans of many friends.

Though the exhibition misses perfection by one per cent, this is somewhat offset by the inclusion of a number of books earlier than those in the original show. That contained Howard's *Songes and Sonettes* in the 1567 edition. We are privileged to display two variant editions of 1559, one Walpole's, the other Bishop Percy's. Of Lyly's *Euphues*, they had the edition of 1581; here is that and a unique one of 1580. Their *Lyrical Ballads* was London; our exhibit has two variants of the Bristol issue. And there are many other such examples. These books were not in the original Grolier show simply because there were probably none in America at that time, a vivid example of the rapid growth of our literary resources.

14
NOTES ON RARITY (1965)

One of Mr. Randall's most successful, and spectacular, exhibits at The Lilly Library was devoted to American poetry. Professor J. Albert Robbins supplied the notes for the catalogue and Randall provided the collations and this perceptive note. [From *Three Centuries of American Poetry: An Exhibition of Original Printings.* Bloomington: Indiana University, The Lilly Library, 1965, pp. vi-viii.]

THIS exhibition of original editions of American poetry and verse is drawn almost entirely from the resources of the Lilly Library. No such comprehensive showing has ever been done before. *The Bay Psalm Book*, the first book printed within the boundaries of the United States, has been lent by the Rosenbach Foundation, Philadelphia, Pennsylvania, and a dozen uncommon books, identified in the catalogue, range from the first American edition of Anne Bradstreet's *Several Poems* (Boston, 1670) to William Carlos William's *Poems* (Rutherford, N.J., 1909), by H. Bacon Collamore of West Hartford, Connecticut, whose collection of American poetry is the most distinguished in private hands. All others demonstrate J.K. Lilly's life-long interest in poetry, and it should be noted that, in some ways, his collection of English poetry is more comprehensive than is his American.

Volumes of poetry, especially first volumes, are fragile barks and many of the books shown are *introuvables*. The wonder is that some have survived at all. No copy is known of the original printing of Michael Wigglesworth's *The Day of Doom* (probably London, 1662), and to skip three centuries, Robert Frost's first production, *Twilight* (Lawrence, Massachusetts, 1894), has survived, in a single copy, in the Barrett collection at the University of Virginia, although it is only fair to point out that only two copies were printed to begin with. The place of original publication and the date of so noted a poem as Bryant's *Thanatopsis* is still in doubt. And absolutely nothing is known of the circumstances surrounding the printing and the suppression of Edgar Allan Poe's first book, *Tamerlane* (Boston, 1827), the most sought for and valuable of all American volumes of poetry.

A few poets never achieved publication during their lifetime. Edward Taylor (1642-1729), now recognized as the most important American poet of his era, has set some sort of record for this, none of his poems appearing until 1939. And Emily Dickinson saw only one of her poems in a book while she lived--and then it appeared anonymously and most people attributed it to Ralph Waldo Emerson. Several noted poets never issued a volume of poetry at all. Thoreau, for example, scattered his poems through his prose works. Although Oliver Wendell Holmes did issue volumes of poetry, several of his best known works, such as "The Chambered Nautilus" and "The Deacon's Masterpiece," appear in *The Autocrat of the Breakfast Table* (Boston, 1858), and passages from Thomas Wolfe's prose have been rearranged into poetry, viz., *A Stone, A Leaf, A Door*, by John S. Barnes, published with a foreword by Louis Untermeyer (New York, 1945).

A surprising number of American poets had their first works published abroad. Our very first poet, Anne Bradstreet, is the earliest example, and our first Negro poet, again a woman, Phyllis Wheatley, *Poems* (London, 1773), is another. In the next century, aside from two extremely rare pamphlets printed in Oregon in 1868 and 1869 and both represented in this exhibition, Cincinnatus Hiner Miller found his audience for his next three books in England: *Pacific Poems* and also *Songs of the Sierras* were both published in London in 1871, and *Songs of the Sun Lands* in the same city in 1873, about as far from the scenes they celebrate as it is possible to get. And many lesser known nineteenth century American poets first saw English publication.

There is a virtual rash of twentieth-century names. Elinor Wylie's anonymous first book, *Incidental Numbers* (London, 1912), and her last, *Angels and Earthly Creatures* (Henley-on-Thames, 1928), were privately printed in editions of sixty and fifty-one copies, respectively. Robert Frost's first two books were published in England: *A Boy's Will* (London, 1913) and *North of Boston*

(London, 1914), as was T.S. Eliot's first, *Prufrock* (London, 1917). Among American authors whose works were first published in Europe are Ezra Pound's *A Lume Spento* (Venice, Italy, 1909) and Ernest Hemingway's *Three Stories and Ten Poems* (Dijon, France, 1923).

The work of a few poets first appeared when they were getting along in years (as poets go, that is). Ralph Waldo Emerson's *Poems* (Boston, 1847) appeared when he was forty-four years old, and both Walt Whitman and James Whitcomb Riley were thirty-six when *Leaves of Grass* (Brooklyn, 1855) and *The Old Swimmin'-hole* (Indianapolis, 1883) were published.

However, the initial volumes of most poets appear when they are fairly young. Few, though, were as young as Nathalia Crane when her smash success, *The Janitor's Boy* (New York, 1924), was issued and went rapidly through six editions. She was ten and one half and had been writing since the age of eight.

Family pride accounts for the publication of many works. Our own very first poet, Anne Bradstreet, was printed because her admiring brother-in-law saw to it that her works were published in England in 1650. William Cullen Bryant's father was so pleased with his offspring's talent that he published his *The Embargo* as "By a Youth of Thirteen" (Boston, 1808), followed by a second edition under the author's name the following year, a copy of which is exhibited. The poet was later so ashamed of this vicious satire on Jefferson that he never allowed it to appear in his published works though he survived it for sixty-nine years.

William Rose Benét sponsored the work of his younger brother, Stephen Vincent, *Five Men and Pompey* (Boston, 1915), which was eventually remaindered. Edith Newbold Jones's father had her *Verses* privately printed at Newport, Rhode Island, in 1878, when she was sixteen for presentation to family and friends. Perhaps five copies have survived and it has never been reprinted. Its author, Edith Wharton, went on to fame as a novelist.

But many an aspiring young poet, sans family support, has financed his own work. Poe's *Tamerlane* (Boston, 1827) was published when the author was eighteen. This "black tulip" which survives in twelve copies, not all perfect, was a truly juvenile effort. The Preface reads: "The greater part of the Poems which compose this little volume were written in the year 1821-2, when the author had not completed his fourteenth year. They were of course not intended for publication; why they are now published concerns no one but himself." When the poem was reprinted in his second volume, *Al Aaraaf* (Baltimore, 1829), it was with the: "Advertisement. This poem (Tamerlane) was printed for publication in Boston, in the year 1827, but suppressed through circumstances of a private nature." The mystery, if it is ever solved, will probably turn out to be that Poe simply couldn't pay the printer of whom nothing is known except that he, too, was eighteen and is not known to have printed another book.

William Carlos Williams financed his first privately printed *Poems* (Rutherford, N.J., 1909) and sold four copies at 25 cents each. A copy was recently offered for sale at $1,700. Eleven are known but only two of the first issue, before numerous errors were corrected. This makes it runner-up to Frost's *Twilight* in the twentieth-century American poetry rarity sweepstakes. Most of the edition was destroyed when the henhouse in which the printer stored it was burned. And Williams paid a London firm $50 in 1913 to issue his first published work, *The Tempers*. Robinson Jeffers' bibliographer relates that his first book, *Flagons and Apples* (Los Angeles, 1912), "was published entirely at the author's expense in an edition of 500 copies at $1. . . Of the 500 copies printed, R.J. left 480 with the printer; of the twenty copies he took he gave away three or four and burned the rest. The printer subsequently sold the 480 remaining copies to a secondhand bookstore for twenty cents a copy." Edwin Arlington Robinson financed his initial effort, *The Torrent and the Night Before* (Gardiner, Maine, 1896), to the tune of $52 for 312 copies, all of which he gave away, suitably inscribed. Fifty-six are known to have survived, a high percentage as these things go.

Some of the books exhibited were printed for surprising reasons. H.L. Mencken's *Ventures into Verse* (Baltimore, 1903), appeared because some friends wanted a publication to display some new type and a small volume of poetry was cheaper to print than a large volume of prose. *In Reckless Ecstasy* (Galesburg, Ill., 1904), "By Charles A. Sandburg," was printed because a friend had a printing press in his cellar and wanted to use it.

College graduations have furnished springboards for some poets. We are not quite sure how James Russell Lowell celebrated his election as class poet. We do know that, as one biographer puts it, he went to chapel when he should have gone to bed. He was rusticated by the Harvard faculty to the neighboring town of Concord "until the Saturday before Commencement," and was thus prevented from reading his *Class Poem* (Cambridge, 1838), which was then published anonymously in a pamphlet of thirty-nine pages. Archibald MacLeish's Yale *Class Poem* (New Haven, 1915), a four-page leaflet, precedes his first published book by two years, and Edna St. Vincent Millay's first separately published poem when she was at Vassar was the "Baccalaureate Hymn," issued to the appropriate tune, "St. Vincent," and signed "Words and Music Edna St. Vincent Millay, '17." It was first issued as a broadside (Poughkeepsie, N.Y., 1917).

Many writers whose fame rests chiefly on their prose began as poets, or at least their first publications were poetry. Among these are Frank Norris, *Yvernelle* (Philadelphia, 1892); George Santayana, *Sonnets and Other Verse* (Cambridge and Chicago, 1894); Willa Cather, *April Twilights* (Boston, 1903); Glenway Westcott, *The Bitterns* (Evanston, Ill., 1920); and William Faulkner, *The Marble Faun* (Boston, 1924). Some others, as Sinclair Lewis and Theodore Dreiser, were writing poetry for magazines before their prose appeared in print.

But, lest we forget it, a goodly number of people simply wrote their poetry, had it published, and received royalties, right from the start. . . .

15

THE ADVENTURE OF THE NOTORIOUS FORGER (1946)

While he was not a charter member of The Baker Street Irregulars, David Randall was an enthusiastic reader of A. Conan Doyle and a great supporter of the Sherlock Holmes stories. For a time he edited the bibliographical notes section of "The Baker Street Journal" to which he contributed this theoretical piece on Holmes and Thomas J. Wise. [From The Baker Street Journal, 1 (July, 1946):371-377.]

MOST of us have at least a passing knowledge of the exploits of the late Thomas J. Wise, Honorary Master of Arts at Oxford University, Honorary Fellow of Worcester College, Oxford, Member of the Roxburghe Club (the most exclusive institution of book collectors in the world), President of the English Bibliographical Society from 1922 to 1924, assembler of the famed Ashley Library, one of the greatest ever formed in England, now a part of the British Museum -- and at the same time the most successful forger the world has ever known.

His fantastic exploits were exposed in a sensational book entitled *An Enquiry into the Nature of Certain Nineteenth Century Pamphlets*, by John Carter and Graham Pollard, published in 1934. In that volume more than fifty valuable "first editions" by such eminent authors as Wordsworth, Tennyson, Dickens, Thackeray, the Brownings, Swinburne, Kipling, George Eliot, Stevenson, and others were shown to be fakes manufactured by Wise. Carter and Pollard's classic work is one of the great detective feats of all time, and the object of this paper is not to detract from their accomplishments but to supplement them by telling for the first time the true story of Thomas James Wise, his nemeses (Carter and Pollard) and the part Sherlock Holmes played in all this.

For does anyone think this forger, Wise, could have flourished as Sherlock's contemporary without the detective's knowing about him -- and, more, frustrating him? "If such there breathe, go, mark him well;" he simply doesn't know his Holmes. Truly interpreted, the Sacred Writings as revealed, somewhat inadequately, by Watson, contain the complete story of the epic struggle of Holmes to defeat Wise. A little of this struggle I will reveal here, dealing only in facts and drawing no conclusions not justified by the evidence contained in the canon. Watson, of course, could not, English libel laws being what they are, tell the story without disguising some names and places, but he left blatantly obvious signs for us to follow.

First, let us consider a little chronology. One of the crucial periods of Wise's life was the year 1886 when he founded the Shelley Society. This respectable front got him into touch with the firm of Clay, printers, who did legitimate Shelley facsimile work for the Society. Later, when Wise had other not-so-legitimate work, Clay, used to his odd requests, did that for him also. Wise had begun his career of besmirching revered names, unsuspected, he thought, by anyone.

But what was Holmes doing in 1886? In *The Hound of the Baskervilles* he stated on September 29, 1886: ". . . at the present instant one of the most revered names in England is being besmirched. . . and only I can stop a disastrous scandal." And what about this Clay in whose "Long Primer" so many of Wise's forgeries were printed?

In *The Red-Headed League* Holmes dubs him "the third or fourth smartest man in London." "He's a remarkable man, is young John Clay. His grandfather was a royal duke and he himself has been to Eton and Oxford. His brain is as cunning as his fingers." I could go into this Clay business at more length but, out of respect for a revered BSI member, I refrain for the following reason. Holmes expresses (in the *Adventure of the Empty House*) a theory that "the individual represents in his development the whole procession of his ancestors, and a sudden turn to good or evil stands for some strong influence that came into the line of his pedigree. The person becomes, as it were, the epitome of the history of his own family." It would be scarcely cricket to elaborate this thesis, since the grandson of that Clay is Christopher Morley!

While we are on the subject of names, let's consider the Smiths. There is a mystery about Wise's first wife, whose maiden name was Smith. According to his biographer, Wilfred Partington (*Forging Ahead*, page 120): "one day in 1895 she stepped out of Thomas's life. . . into the blue." This is the hitherto unrecognized basis of *The Adventure of the Solitary Cyclist* which Watson takes pains to let us know took place in 1895, concerned a Miss Smith, her marriage and disappearance all of which took place near where Holmes "took Archie Stamford, the forger." Incidentally, also, consider the fact that Wise lived in a peculiar part of London--Hampstead--described by no less than E.V. Lucas as "a devilish difficult place to find on a foggy night." Every school child knows that Charles Augustus Milverton, "the worst man in London," "a genius in his way," lived in Hampstead.

All this is by way of bring up the fateful year 1896. It was in that year that Wise's most successful forgery, the so-called "1847 Reading" edition of Mrs. Browning's *Sonnets from the Portuguese* was first announced. Watson left plenty of clues of Holmes' interest in this particular forgery. Some of them are in the *Adventure of the Six Napoleons*. Where did the last and most important of these turn up? Reading, of course.

It was in 1894 that Holmes returned to London and frightened Watson into a faint--Watson who had thought him at the bottom of the Reichenbach Fall the past three years. Now, I ask you to recall: how did Holmes return to London? Let Watson tell the story of the wonderful meeting: "I struck against an elderly deformed man who had been behind me and I knocked down several books which he was carrying. . . .It struck me that the fellow must be some poor bibliophile who, either as a trade or as a hobby, was a collector of obscure volumes." Holmes returned, that is, in the disguise of a secondhand book dealer--the perfect disguise to investigate the newest of Wise's forgeries. An absurd disguise to look into (as Watson intimates) the goings-on of one the Honourable Ronald Adair.

Holmes goes on to say to Watson: "I am a neighbor of yours, for you'll find my little bookshop at the corner of Church Street, and very happy to see you I am sure. Maybe you collect yourself, sir. Here's 'British Birds' and 'The Holy War'--a bargain every one of them."

Now why did Holmes offer those two particular volumes, out of all the millions he could have possessed? Simply because returning to England to investigate Wise, as he did, he naturally had with him some volumes in which the forger also would be interested. Carter and Pollard, *op. cit.*, page 57, explain that one of the key books in the resurrection of "old style" type, the only large-scale innovation in type design that took place in the nineteenth century, was a font used for William Pickering in his edition of Fuller's *Holy War.* This is a vastly important clue in the unmasking of Wise. As to the *British Birds*, I am not quite clear in my own mind if this is a clue hinting at Birdy Edwards of the *Valley of Fear*, or at Wise's favorite fall-guy who bought many of his forgeries (now in the Library of the University of Texas, Austin, Texas)--John Henry *Wrenn*.

One more quotation from the *Adventure of the Empty House*: "If I remember right, you had not heard the name of Professor James Moriarty, who had one of the great brains of the century. Just give me down my index of biographies from the shelf. . . My collection of M's is a fine one," said Holmes. Watson reads the singular dossier on Sebastian Moran--"the second most dangerous man in London"--and comments: "This is astonishing. The man's career is that of an honourable soldier." "It is true," said Holmes, "up to a certain point he did well. There are some trees, Watson, which grow to a certain height, and then develop some unsightly eccentricity. You see it often in humans." This is the prefect description of Wise, and again the clue is there: turn an *M* upside down and you get *W*!

Sherlock's enemies were relentless. As we know, he often went in fear of his life (there were fifty men who sought it) and there were many attempts on it. No wonder he took precautions to protect himself. His *indices* were precious, so he evolved his own filing system. Things were not where an intruder would expect to find them. Remember *The Adventure of the Sussex Vampire* and, again a *forger*, Victor Lynch? Holmes catalogued him in his index under *V*. And what does that tell us? Well, what is the letter following *V*? *W*! Wise.

Now, referring to Wise's biographer (Partington, *op. cit.*, page 116), Wise's "wild career" continued from the age of 27 to about 40. As Wise was born in 1859, his forgeries began in 1886 and ended about 1901, and were concentrated in the final half decade of the last century. His activities coincided exactly, that is, with Holmes' most active period. In *The Adventure of the Solitary Cyclist*, Watson tells us that "From the years 1894" (that is, when Holmes returned to London) "to 1901" (no Wise forgeries are known after that date) "Mr. Sherlock Holmes was a very busy man. It is safe to say that there was no public case of any difficulty in which he was not consulted and there were hundreds of private cases, some of the most intricate and extraordinary character, in which he played a prominent part."

We have already considered the first crucial year, 1886--Wise-Clay versus Holmes. We have considered the second crucial year, 1894, when Wise attempted his first "big-time" forgery and Holmes returned from abroad to confound him. Let us take the next year, 1895. What happened in 1895? Well, let us look at the record: Watson tells us in *The Adventure of the Three Students* that "it was in the year '95 that a combination of events, into which I shall not enter, caused Mr. Sherlock Holmes and myself to spend some weeks in one of our great university towns. It will be obvious that any details which would help the reader to identify exactly the college or the criminal would be injudicious and offensive. So painful a scandal may well be allowed to die. . . We were residing at the time in furnished lodgings *close to a library* where Sherlock Holmes was pursuing some laborious researches."

Now what was Wise doing in 1895? Well, in that year he issued a catalogue: *The Ashley Library, A List of Books Printed for Private Circulation* and the first volume of his and Nicoll's *Literary Anecdotes of the Nineteenth Century*. No wonder the checking of that "combination of events" led Holmes to a research job in the only place such research could be conducted--the library of a "great university town." Holmes, one must remember, was a great bibliographer. Watson tells us in *The Red-Headed League* that Holmes was "never so formidable as when, for days on end, he had been lounging in his armchair amid his black-letter editions." Recall, again, that one of Carter and Pollard's most potent weapons in exposing Wise was the fact that Wise used the wrong kind of paper for the books he forged. In *A Scandal in Bohemia* Holmes reveals his expert knowledge of the composition of paper (which he knew as well as he did tobacco ashes) when he remarks, casually: "It is not an English paper at all." And he was right.

Let us consider only a few of the innumerable hints Watson gives us of the Holmes-Wise struggle. Holmes had few close friends, and there were even fewer people he admired. One of these was Lord Roberts (vide The Adventure of the Blanched Soldier). This is the Roberts who, in the Fortnightly Review, March, 1894, attacked a bibliographer (Slater, a friend of Wise's), Wise replying in the following issue. It is obvious that anyone, in 1894, who attacked Wise or a satellite of his would be a friend of Holmes. Slater, by the way, appears in the case of Black Peter, one recalls, as a stone-mason who first noticed the "goings-on at Black Peter's cabin." We could go on endlessly, but we have established enough facts for even the most skeptical.

To recapitulate: The careers of Thomas J. Wise, forger extraordinary, and Sherlock Holmes, detective even more extraordinary, coincided chronologically, as we have seen. Holmes retired in 1901 and there are no Wise forgeries after that date. This poses the problem: Why was Holmes satisfied with his antagonist's retirement from forgery, upon merely a stalemate? Why did Watson go to such lengths to indicate, while never daring fully to reveal, the whole story? And why did it finally come out?

The answer is very simple. Ronald Knox came close to the truth in his brilliant "The Mystery of Mycroft," and A.G. Macdonell had a hint in his "Mr. Moriarty." We know very little of Mycroft; Holmes himself discouraged research in his direction: "I could not have believed that you would have descended to this. You have made inquiries into the history of my unhappy brother." Holmes also once admitted: "Some of my most interesting cases have come to me. . . through Mycroft." Watson knew Holmes's brother "held some small office under the British Government"--an understatement, as we know, from The Adventure of the Bruce-Partington Plans that Mycroft held a position so important that, occasionally, he was the British government.

Moriarty-Moran-Wise: all were Mycroft. Holmes was never vindictive, even to his most deadly opponents. The game was the thing--punishment was generally another's duty. He admired his brother tremendously, and we have Holmes' word that "Mycroft's talents were superior to his own." So when he forced Mycroft to abandon his literary forgeries and turn his talents to His Majesty's Intelligence Service, Holmes retired.

But he left documentary evidence of the sordid story in competent hands--those of Graham Pollard, Watson's son by his second wife, and to his own son, John Carter. This story was to be held as a threat over Mycroft's head should he ever reveal another "sudden turn to evil."

We are now treading on delicate ground--English libel laws being strict. This much we can reveal: Mycroft-Moran-Wise-Holmes changed his name when he gave up forgery. This is a matter of record and can be checked in *Living Authors* (H.W. Wilson, 1935) where one finds him (John Carter's uncle, remember) listed as having "assumed the original family name of his ancestors, a branch of the Mackenzie clan of Scotwell;" he acted as Director of Intelligence in Ethiopia in 1917 and later as Intelligence Control Officer of a Balkan nation. Honorably retired, he reverted to earlier criminal tendencies (or perhaps he was merely ill-advised by some publisher) and wrote a book which caused questions to be asked in Parliament and was threatened with prosecution under the War Secrets Act. The famous *Enquiry* was published, I sincerely believe, to reveal his early history, discredit him, and forestall any steps he may have contemplated taking to fight the suppression of his war scandals. I think he knew when he was licked and was again content with a stalemate and there, let, as we shall, the whole matter drop.

16 - 19
BIBLIOGRAPHICAL
NOTES AND QUERIES

Throughout his career David Randall contributed to the notes and queries columns of several journals, including "The Baker Street Journal," Elkin Mathews' "Bibliographical Notes & Queries," "The Book Collector," and the "Papers of the Bibliographical Society of America." Reprinted here are four representative examples of this work.

16

[A. Conan Doyle] [From the *Papers of the Bibliographical Society of America*, 34 (Second Quarter, 1940): 190-191.]

DOYLE, A. Conan (1879-1928). Memoirs | Of | Sherlock Holmes | By | A. Conan Doyle | Author of "Adventures of Sherlock Holmes" | "The Refugees" "Micah Clarke" Etc. | Illustrated | (Publishers' device) | New York | Harper & Brothers Publishers | 1894 |.

Collation: (a)^4, (A)-S^8. Size: 7 1/4 x 5 7/8 inches.

Contents: Endpaper; [i-ii] blank; frontispiece (inserted); [iii] title-page, as above; [iv] Copyright, 1893, by A. Conan Doyle. | (Rule) | Copyright, 1894, by

Harper & Brothers. | (Rule) | All rights reserved.; [v] Contents; [vi] blank; [vii-viii (the last misnumbered vi)] Illustrations; 1-251, text; [282] blank; [283-288] advertisements; endpaper.

Illustrations: Frontispiece and twenty-five others, all inserted.

Binding: Blue mesh cloth. Front cover stamped in black with an elaborate design, and gilt lettered and ruled beneath this: Memoirs | Of | Sherlock Holmes | (Rule) | A Conan Doyle |. Back cover blank. Spine gilt lettered and ruled with ornament stamped in black: Memoirs | Of | Sherlock | Holmes | (Rule) | Doyle | Harpers |.
First American Edition.

Note: The second edition contains 259 pages of text, only, has the words: New and Revised Edition on the title-page, and differs in other particulars.

The first edition is a book of considerable importance as it contains the first printing in book form of The Cardboard Box which was omitted from the English Edition of the Memoirs and was not issued again in either country until 1917 when it turned up in The Case Book. Doyle tells, in his autobiography, that he refused to print The Cardboard Box in the Memoirs (it first appeared in The Strand Magazine, January, 1893) because he came to regard it as an affront to pure womanhood and felt that Holmes' allusions to the misdemeanours of the lady might lead someone astray. Harpers, in reprinting the stories from The Strand Magazine, unwittingly included The Cardboard Box, and, upon Doyle's immediate protests, withdrew the edition and reprinted the book omitting it.

17

[W. M. Thackeray] [From the *Papers of the Bibliographical Society of America*, 34 (Second Quarter, 1940): 191-192.]

THACKERAY, W.M. (1811-1863). Vanity Fair. 20 parts in 19. London, 1847-1848.

It has long been noted that the last four parts of <u>Vanity Fair</u> occur with the front wrapper sometimes dated, sometimes undated; and with the bracket after the volume number and before the word "Price," present in some copies, absent in others. However, so far as I know, no general examination of the problems presented has been undertaken by anyone.

Examination of these parts reveals clearly that the undated parts are not merely the same as the dated parts with only the date omitted, but are entirely reset. There are numerous differences but the following are typical:

(a) The dated parts xvi-xviii measure vertically, within the outer border rules, approximately 7 13/16 inches; the undated parts 7 11/16 inches.

(b) The subtitle, <u>Pen and Pencil Sketches of English Society</u> measures, from the capital P to the final period, approximately 4 inches in the dated parts; 1/8 inch less in the undated.

It should be noted, for what it is worth, that the measurements of the dated parts from xvi on are closer to those of parts ii-xv than are those of the undated parts.

The final part, a double one, xix-xx, exists both dated and undated, and with, in addition, variant imprints. Up to and including part xviii, the imprint is: London: | Published At The Punch Office, 85, Fleet Street. | J. Menzies, Edinburgh; J. McLeod, Glasgow; J. McGlashan, Dublin.

Part xix-xx has the imprint, in dated copies: London: | Published at the Punch Office, 85, Fleet Street. | J. Menzies, Edinburgh; Thos. Murray, Glasgow; J. McGlashan, Dublin.; while in undated copies the imprint is the same except that for Thos. Murray, Glasgow;, the reading is T. Murray, Glasgow;. All of the parts, incidentally, are printed by Bradbury & Evans.

The brackets noted above, after the number and before the word "Price," are absent in some of the dated copies, present in some of the undated ones.

The evidence, therefore, is clear that the wrappers of at least the last four parts of <u>Vanity Fair</u> exist in two forms. Whether these are states or issues is uncertain on the present evidence. The parts are so scarce that additional information from owners as to the measurement of their parts, either dated or undated; of the presence or absence of the brackets; and of the imprints on the final part, would be most welcome. Copies with contemporary inscriptions should be most closely noted. The question of the wrappers is, incidentally, only one of several perplexing problems connected with <u>Vanity Fair</u>. . . .

18

"Bruce Rogers' First Decorated Book" [From the *Papers of the Bibliographical Society of America*, 55 (First Quarter, 1961): 40-42.]

T HE state of Maine, a long way from Indiana, has always been credited with the earliest book in which Bruce Rogers, Hoosier-born printer and book designer, had any part. This is the Thomas Mosher edition of "A.E." (George Russell's) *Homeward Songs by the Way*, Portland, Maine, 1895. It was identified as the first of his "incunabula" in an article by Percy L. Babington--"The First Book Decorated by Mr. Bruce Rogers," in *The Library* v (Fourth Series, No. 2, Sept., 1924), 171, and his attribution has never been challenged.

Mr. Babington states, "seven designs and headbands are his and Mr. Rogers told me himself that here was his earliest work." Such a statement should settle matters, but as the experienced in such matters know, it often doesn't. *Homeward Songs* remains the earliest book signed by the familiar "BR," but it is not, by two years, the first book decorated by him.

This, appropriately, is a book printed in Indianapolis and recently identified in The Lilly Library, Indiana University, and as Alice said even "curiouser," is a work done for the Eli Lilly Company.

It is an oblong booklet, 8 x 5 inches, of 10 unnumbered leaves on coated paper, printed on verso only, bound in cream-colored wrappers with gold-colored ties, lettered (with a mortar design in gold) on the front wraper. It is enclosed in an envelope, lettered in purple, *Botany in Pharmacy*.

This title is repeated on the cover. There is no title-page. The first page has, between rules: By John S. Wright, | Botanical Department | Eli Lilly & Company.

Apparently only two copies of this pamphlet are known at this writing. One is in the files of the Eli Lilly Company and one is in The Lilly Library.

The evidence for its attribution to Rogers is a letter to J. K.

Lilly, Jr., dated 3 Dec. 1940, from the author, John S. Wright, presenting him with a copy and reading in part:

> The hand-lettered title, initial "B," the scrolls around the halftone cuts and the tail piece are by Bruce Rogers, engraved by the old Indiana Illustrating Company. This company was founded by Earl E. Stafford about 1893 with an office in the old Cyclorama building, where the Traction Terminal and "Bus" sheds are now.
>
> Last night I called Earl E. Stafford and he said Rogers worked for him in 1893 when he was in this vicinity. At the time your father and I called Rogers was just beginning to feel normal after a slow convalescence from an appendectomy, a rare operation in "them days."
>
> Stafford's recollection confirms my own so it would appear that the drawings were made in or about March, 1893. I remember our call on Rogers was in warm or mild weather.

The company mentioned is long out of existence and it is not known what other work Rogers did for them. He records, in *Who's Who*, however (a fact no one seems hitherto to have noticed), that he was "Designer for Ind. Illustrating Co., 1893-4." He also records in the same volume that he was associated with the famous lithographers "L. Prang & Co. Boston, 1894-5," but none of his work for them has yet been identified.

The Lilly advertising brochure, therefore, seems to qualify as Number I in the Bruce Rogers check-lists.

19

"Query 267. Ian Fleming's First Book" [From *The Book Collector*, 21 (Autumn, 1972): 414-415.]

What appears to be Fleming's first book has just come to light in the course of the transfer of his papers to the Lilly Library, Indiana University at Bloomington. Its title-page is KEMSLEY / NEWSPAPERS/ . /REFERENCE / BOOK / KEMSLEY HOUSE LONDON-ENGLAND, it consists of 58 leaves, 5" x 3", inserted in a two-ring binder (Walker's 'Ready' Ring Book No. 5913).

The contents consists of a manual of useful information for members of the staff of Kemsley Newspapers Ltd., under the following headings: Kemsley Newspapers, Foreign Department, Memorandum to Empire and Foreign Correspondents, Preparation of Telegrams, Edition Times, Deadlines, Comparison of World Times, Key Industries, Newspapers Circulating throughout Great Britain, Provincial Newspapers, Scottish Newspapers, Welsh Newspapers, Map, Population, Net Sales, Telegraphic Addresses, Subscription Rates Abroad, Calendar, Glossary of Printing and Newspaper Terms, Notes.

In the copy in the Lilly Library, the text is paginated 1-126 pages, but after page 10 there is a leaf inserted with 'Pages 11-20 inclusive In Course of Preparation' printed on the recto (verso blank). After page 126 is a leaf advertising Walker's 'Ready' Ring Book followed by 10 leaves of blank ruled paper. Page 117 has a *Calendar for 1949*, probably the year it was issued. Done primarily for the guidance of Foreign Correspondents the verso of the title-page bears the name of the recipient (in this case Patrick Henry) and a note that 'In the event of the holder leaving the service of Kemsley Newspapers, this book must be returned'.

It would be interesting to know if any other copies survive, and, in particular whether any contain the text of pp. 11-20.

20 - 24

BOOK REVIEWS

Not only was Mr. Randall a prolific reviewer of books, especially in the early days of his career, but he reviewed some of the most important books in the fields of bibliography and book collecting. His reviews appeared in "Publishers' Weekly," "The Book Collector," the "Papers of the Bibliographical Society of America," the "New York Times Book Review," and elsewhere. Five examples are reprinted here.

20

"A Bibliographical Sensation."   Review of *An Enquiry into the Nature of Certain Nineteenth Century Pamphlets*, by John Carter and Graham Pollard. [From *Publishers' Weekly*, 126 (July 7, 1934): 54-56.]

T HE booktrade the past two years, and the newspapers the past two months, have been buzzing with rumors of the probable contents of this amazing book. It was known that Carter and Pollard had been working for some little time upon certain suspected 19th Century pamphlets and had uncovered evidence casting doubts upon the authenticity of, primarily, Mrs. Browning's Sonnets from the Portuguese (Sonnets by E. B. B., Reading, 1847), and secondarily upon a group of other pamphlets. No one, however, knew more than the vaguest details. Now the entire investigation is unfolded in a book which is a mixture of detective story and process verbal, with a dash of McKerrow and some notable prisoners in the dock.

This volume is by all odds the bibliographical sensation of the modern bookcollecting era, and the story gains added interest by the clever presentation of the evidence, damning with masterly understatement. There have been forgeries before in the book world, and more in the literary world, but no one ever contemplated even the remotest possibility of such wholesale and successful perpetration of fraud as is here uncovered. It took a genius (there is no other name for the unnamed protagonist of this drama) to successfully produce fifty fakes, provenence them, market them, and completely defy detection over a period of more than a generation.

It is certain that the publication of this book, uncovering and publicizing such fraud, will have important and far-reaching consequences in the rare book world. The immediate damage may well be rather serious, both directly and indirectly, for as the authors themselves realize and state, the uncovering of such spectacular fraud has dealt the honorable science of bibliography a blow "the repercussions of which will be long and widely felt." The book is due to cause acrimonious controversy in which sides will be taken, and the reviewer may here state his own views, personal and minor though they may be. He is (he hopes) on the side of the angels in feeling that the authors have done what will prove eventually of inestimable service to the rare book trade in laboriously, systematically, and scientifically unravelling these frauds, thoroughly documenting every step of their research. They have introduced scientific method never applied to bibliography before and have proved conclusively, not how easy it is to invent or fabricate pamphlets but how difficult it is to do so without detection once suspicion is aroused.

Not that, of course, one need be, in the future, an expert qualitative chemist, trained typefounder, or authority upon paper-making before undertaking to sell rare books; but the aid of such experts is necessary in solving certain bibliographical problems instead of depending, as has been the case only too often heretofore, upon the "look" or "feel" of an item, or upon intuition. The present volume shows conclusively the startling need of such exact knowledge and scientific method, and in going all out for it, and distributing laurels, one must remember the enormous amount of labor which every paragraph shows, and that practically all the data upon type faces and paper manufacture, their dates of introduction, etc., dug out by the authors, are pioneer work.

But to return to the book proper. It details too intricate and manysided an investigation to be other than briefly summarized here. Anyone with the slightest interest in bibliography owes it to himself to purchase and read the volume for its genuine intellectual fascination. Briefly, it is divided into three parts, Deduction, Reconstruction and Dossiers. The Deduction gives the story of the origin and various stages of the investigation. First was the accumulation of negative evidence against the authenticity of certain pamphlets, among them the "Sonnets." The absence of any particle of reliable contemporary evidence for their printing or existence before their discovery (the "Sonnets" was "discovered" in 1886), the fact that it, and others linked with it, never appeared with presentation inscriptions, or indeed contemporary inscriptions of any kind, and much like evidence, told heavily against their authenticity.

But positive evidence which could be interpreted to some definite conclusion was necessary. So the paper and type of the suspected pamphlets were examined carefully and critically by competent authorities. Briefly what was discovered was that any paper containing esparto (the first successful substitute for rags in paper making), must have been manufactured after 1861 at the earliest, and any paper containing chemical wood, after 1874. Application of this test to the suspected group of pamphlets (dated from 1842 on), proved many of them forgeries.

The typographical analysis showed that many of the suspected pamphlets and (by the paper test) proved forgeries, had common typographical peculiarities, were printed in a particular type of font with a kernless design. Through a laborious, but exciting, piece of research, the authors prove that no such type was extant prior to its casting in 1876 by R. Clay and Sons (who, incidentally, printed the present volume); yet there were many of the pamphlets dated prior to 1876. The authors classify the various text types of the suspected and proved forgeries, and from the paper, type, text, negative evidence, and a combination of all the tests prove pamphlets of some fifteen authors to be "wrong." These authors are, Matthew Arnold, the Brownings, Dickens, Eliot, Kipling, Morris, Rossetti, Ruskin, Stevenson, Swinburne, Tennyson,

Thackeray, Wordsworth and Yates. Among the outright forgeries are:

E.B. Browning. "Sonnets," 1847. "The Runaway Slave," 1849.

Robert Browning. "Cleon," 1855. "The Statue and the Bust," 1855. "Gold Hair," 1864.

Charles Dickens. "To Be Read at Dusk," 1852.

John Ruskin. "The Scythian Guest," 1849.

Charles Swinburne. "Siena," 1868. "Dolores," 1867.

Lord Tennyson. "Morte d'Arthur," 1842. "Lucretius" (Cambridge, Mass., the only cloth bound book in the lot), 1868. "The Last Tournament," 1871.

Among the pirates are:

Rudyard Kipling. "White Horses," 1897. "The White Man's Burden," 1899.

R.L. Stevenson. "The Thermal Influence of Forests," 1873. (This is a piracy of an authentic first, till now generally regarded as a second, i.e., the issue with "From the Proceedings," etc., on the title page).

The list of known forgeries is too long to be detailed here, while quite as important are the pamphlets labelled "highly suspicious." The pamphlets in this group could easily have been called outright forgeries, as in every case the evidence is so strongly against them, as to, to the reader at least, admit of no defence. It is in such cases, again, that the authors give a perfect example of the emphasis of under-statement, and wisely avoid even a hint of suspicion of special pleading. The pamphlets will, of course, be rigidly avoided in the future by the astute collector if a word to the wise is sufficient.

Part II, Reconstruction, explains the state of the first edition market, 1885-1895 and shows why, for example, there is a preponderance of Ruskin and Swinburne forgeries among the lot, for those authors were among the "high spots" of the 90's. The forger's method of establishing and marketing the forgeries is clearly explained. The authors believe, with reason, that one man was probably responsible for all the work. It was necessary for him of course, to have someone spread the news of his "finds," someone whose bibliographical eminence was unassailable, and such a man he found in the person of Thomas J. Wise. "Mr. Wise's gullibility may seem extraordinary today," say the authors, "but it must be remembered that neither the general efficiency of bibliographical scrutiny nor his own experience as a collector were so great forty years ago. -- Yet Mr. Wise seems to have accepted without suspicion what must have been a steady stream of three or four 'remainders' a year for fourteen years; and we have no evidence that he carried out any such inquiry into their origins as common sense, let alone bibliographical duty, plainly demanded."

The authors present plentiful evidence that Mr. Wise disposed of a great number of these pamphlets through Mr. Gorfin, the London bookseller (who aided in the present investigation), and "it is impossible to escape the conclusion that Mr. Wise's zeal for the bibliographical establishing of these books,--had a partly commercial motive; and even if this went side by side with the pride of the discoverer,--the fact that the establishing was done mainly under his own name, while the marketing of the books was carried on largely through agents, gives the whole affair a rather unhappy color."

The authors have some harsh words to say about Mr. Wise, and the reviewer on the basis of their researches, could perhaps supplement this, but the author's summary is sufficient. "His original negligence in authenticating his finds: his purchase of them in bulk and subsequent gradual dispersal of them through commercial channels: his disingenuousness in emphasizing the rarity of books which he knew well were not rare in the strict sense at all--all these things have inflicted damage in plenty on innumerable collectors all over the world, who have for years paid good money--and in some cases a good deal of it--for books which are, in fact, worthless except as curiosities. . . . (Mr. Wise) was deceived where he ought not to have been deceived; and if thirty or so spurious books have been established as genuine by the influence of his authority, how can the credit, not only of his own great mass of bibliographical work, but of much else as well, fail to be seriously shaken? . . . If Mr. Wise, one of the most eminent bibliographers of our time, can be so extensively wrong, who can we be sure is right? In the whole history of book collecting there has been no such wholesale and successful perpetration of fraud as that which we owe to this anonymous forger. It has been converted into an unparalleled blow to the bibliography and literary criticism of the Victorian period by the shocking negligence of Mr. Wise."

The charges against Mr. Wise are doubly justified by the

evidence presented, which has not been gone into in this review. The answer to the more serious questions, that of the essential prestige of bibliography itself, is presented, in the reviewer's opinion, by the present monumental work itself. The authors have pointed out new and fruitful methods which in the future, amplified and expanded and rigorously applied to bibliographical problems, will furnish definite and conclusive answers. The important fact is not that such forgeries have been made, but that they have been uncovered and exposed. If the science of bibliography shows evidence of becoming truly scientific, and it does, new methods of approach and research which from this time forward cannot help being applied will owe their existence to Messrs. Carter and Pollard who have not only posed the problem, but uncovered methods for its final solution. Border line cases still exist, of course, and always have and always will, but it seems impossible that such large scale fraud will ever be successfully put over again.

Part III, Dossiers, presents separately the evidence for and against every one of the suspected pamphlets (incidentally, it should be noted that these forgeries are, as the title of the book indicates pamphlets, and in no case books; only one of the forgeries, Tennyson's "Lucretius," 1868, is in a cloth case). The entire case history of every book is thoroughly gone into, its first discovery, auction records, type, paper, etc., recapitulated.

In conclusion it need only be said that the rare book trade and the science of bibliography are doubly fortunate, not only in the exposure of these forgeries, but in the calm, decisive and conclusive manner in which it has been done and the general manner in which the authors, John Carter and Graham Pollard, have handled the investigation reflects nothing but credit upon themselves, the trade, and bibliography itself.

21

Review of *Suppressed Commentaries on the Wiseian Forgeries. Addendum to an Enquiry*, by William B. Todd. [From *College & Research Libraries*, 31 (July, 1970): 282-283.]

"OF making many books" we are told on good authority (Eccles. 12:12), "there is no end." So it is apparently going to be with the Wise saga. William Todd dedicates this *Addendum*, "To John Carter and Graham Pollard Whose Original Enquiry Will Lead to Endless Addenda on the Work of T.J. Wise."

There have already been a flood of books and articles on the subject since the *Enquiry's* original publication in 1934. An interesting aspect of this phenomenon is the fact that the book itself, though raising great interest in the book collecting world, and printed in a small edition, was a slower seller, taking perhaps two decades to go out of print; and it has not, to this day, seen a second edition.

William Todd here documents "four different campaigns undertaken by American nationals for or against the cause of T.J. Wise," two by Charles Heartman, and the others by Gabriel Wells, both booksellers. In addition, Heartman edited the *American Book Collector* and was a noted gadfly. Texas has acquired his files and correspondence about the magazine, from which Todd usefully reprints and annotates his correspondence with Wise, including a revealing article which Wise wrote (or had written for him) with the important sentences: "My own private opinion is that the Browning Sonnets is not genuine. The question is where did Mr. Forman obtain the 'Remainder' from." This article was never published, as Wise demanded its return, which he got, but not before Heartman retained some sort of copy. Miss Fannie Ratchford had seen this document, as Todd points out in a footnote, but failed to appreciate its significance.

Throughout the article Wise refers to Carter and Pollard as "the authors." In other correspondence I have seen, he called them "sewer rats."

The Gabriel Well's crusade (Todd calls it "folly") to vindicate Wise, which is documented, sprang from reasons not revealed in this *Addendum*.

The Ashley Library was the most spectacular one of the kind of books which were in fashion during the decades it was being formed and there was considerable speculation over its eventual disposal. Wells was, at that depression time, the most active dealer in Americana and the general opinion among his fellow dealers was that his defense of Wise was simply a ploy on his part to ingratiate himself with Mrs. Wise and others so he would be regarded favorably by them when and if an opportunity came along to purchase the collection. The Heartman correspondence with Wise is important to the saga, that of Wells is not.

Todd concludes with a "Postscript on *The Story of a Lie*" which documents Wise's methods of handling potentially dangerous problems, in this case, W.F. Prideaux's forthcoming bibliography of R.L. Stevenson.

The "Notes," of which there are forty-seven, are occasionally inadequate, or inaccurate, where contemporary personages are involved. Wilfred Partington is confused with (presumably) Henry M. Partridge. Certainly Mrs. Gertrude Hills and the equally formidable Leonard L. Mackall could be more satisfactorily identified, and Arthur Swann (of all people!) was not, in 1934, "President of the Swann galleries." He was, at that time, a bookseller and the Swann galleries, with which he never had any connection, was not in existence. These are minor blemishes on an interesting contribution.

22

"American First Editions." Review of *Merle Johnson's American First Editions. Bibliographic Check Lists of the Works of 199 American Authors.* Third Edition, Revised by Jacob Blanck. [From *Publishers' Weekly*, 130 (November 28, 1936): 2108-2109.]

"**M**ERLE Johnson's American First Editions" is now seven years old and, like all good books, is improving with age. The first edition, to which *The Publishers' Weekly* had previously given serial publication, was issued in 1929, and contained check lists of the works of one hundred and five American authors. Although not a new departure in American bibliography (the compiler gratefully acknowledged his indebtedness to the pioneer work of that Boston sage, P.K. Foley, whose "American Authors" was published in 1897), it proved so useful that an enlarged edition, listing one hundred and forty-six authors and correcting the more obvious errors of the previous volume, was issued in 1932.

From that time until his death in 1935, Merle Johnson planned and worked on another revision of his book, which had become in the few years since its publication an absolutely indispensable ready-reference tool to everyone interested in American "firsts." It is our good fortune that his work was carried on and supplemented by his capable assistant, Jacob Blanck, to whose ability and researches many of the improvements of the second edition were due.

The present edition, the third, "enlarged and corrected," has just been published and contains bibliographic check lists of the works of one hundred and ninety-nine authors, adding fifty-three to the last edition. It is a substantially bound, well-printed volume with ample margins, omits the brief sketches preceding the listing of the various authors' works which were printed in the earlier editions (an omission thoroughly justified, in our opinion, in a reference work of this type), and has a number of blank pages, useful for reference notes, bound in at the end.

A number of new discoveries are recorded, but not as many as some might expect. A comparison with the 1932 edition of the authors common to each, lends little support to the theory that new bibliographic discoveries are becoming so common that collectors, discouraged with finding their prize books "wrong," are justified in abandoning collecting. A new "Alice of Old Vincennes" (with the running heads in bold-face upper case type) is, probably correctly, designated as a "trial issue"; "Penrod," in the "first state of the sheets has p. viii so numbered"; the second issue of Whitman's "The Wound Dresser" has an 1898 copyright date; the variant bindings on Beebe's "Two Bird-Lovers in Mexico" are finally classified (the first has *Charles M. Beebe* on the front cover); the puzzle of issues of Trowbridge's "Cudjo's Cave" is resolved, and other points as now first recorded.

It should be noted to his credit that Mr. Blanck has not rushed into print announcing, with loud hurrahs and the authority that publication in such an institution as this book has become confers, dubious "points" and debatable discoveries. He has avoided dogmatism wherever possible and newly discovered variants (as in Henry James' "The Sacred Fount" and "The Better Sort"), are noted with the properly noncommittal phrase "no priority known." Bibliography is a living science, and as more collectors and dealers exchange notes and compare collations, and as books are more critically examined, discoveries of greater or lesser importance are bound to be made and when made they should be recorded. But only too often in the past "points" have been announced which a little investigation showed to be of no issue importance whatsoever (as the repeated running head at page 363 in Hergesheimer's "The Three Black Pennys"); or variations have been noted from which entirely erroneous conclusions have been drawn, and one is thankful that Mr. Blanck has not dignified, by inclusion in the present work, anything that is not fairly susceptible of objective proof.

Of course, a few errors and omissions are inevitable in a work of this size (there are, probably, over 7500 entries). The imprint of Hugh Brackenridge's "Modern Chivalry," Volume 4 (1797), is Pittsburgh, not Philadelphia; the large-paper editions of several of Dorothy Parker's books are not listed; nor is there any edition of Field's "Little Book of Western Verse" (Chicago, 1889), other than the large paper copies. Poe's "Tales of the Grotesque and Arabesque" has the erroneous note: two copies have been noted with p. 231 misnumbered but the status of these copies is undetermined." The first part of this note should read: "Some (at least three) copies have been noted with page 213 of Volume II, misnumbered 231," and, too, it is now fairly well determined, as comparison of copies has shown, page 213 of Volume II has the numerals progressively out of alignment, that the earlier states have page 213 correctly numbered and that the numerals fell out and were incorrectly replaced in the later state.

However, there are fewer errors, as has been said, than would be expected, and, in Mr. Blanck's revision, "Merle Johnson's American First Editions" remains the most useful reference work upon the average dealers' and collectors' bibliographical shelf. It is to be hoped that Mr. Blanck will continue to compare, note, collate, revise and enlarge, and at some future date furnish us with still another edition. It would be most helpful if dealers would write to him, as a sort of clearing house for news bibliographical, and if, at various times, "points" could be discussed and new discoveries considered in the pages of The Publishers' Weekly to whose enterprise and encouragement all the editions of "American First Editions" owe so much.

Typographically the volume is patterned after the edition of

1932. For more ready reference the running heads have been printed at the fore-edge corners, an innovation that simplifies the use of the volume.

In addition to the regular library edition the publishers issued a small number of copies on thin paper in semi-flexible binding, designed for travelers and scouts who find a smaller volume more convenient.

23

Review of *Bibliographical Resources for the Study of Nineteenth Century English Fiction* by Gordon N. Ray. [From the *Papers of the Bibliographical Society of America*, 59 (Second Quarter, 1965): 208-211.]

T HE fourth of the Zeitlin & Ver Brugge Lectures in Bibliography was given at UCLA, 4 May 1964, by Dr. Gordon N. Ray and was entitled "Bibliographical Resources for the Study of Nineteenth Century English Fiction." Dr. Ray is equally distinguished as a scholar and a book collector in this century and his choice of subject was a happy one. A great deal of careful preparation went into his paper which is emphatically not a glib report based on airy generalities.

He records the results of a questionnaire sent to twenty-seven libraries, six in England, two in Scotland, one in Ireland, eighteen in America, and four (unnamed) private collectors and comments, too briefly, on them.

The questionnaire requested details of holdings of 130 selected books, asking specifically whether the books were in original state or rebound. There were seven categories: (1) First editions of fiction by major novelists, thirty titles; (2) First editions of fiction by secondary novelists, forty titles; (3) First editions of fiction by occasional novelists, twenty titles; (4) First editions of fiction published in parts, ten titles; (5) Later editions of fiction important for textual reasons, twelve titles; (6) Magazines in which fiction was first serialized, ten titles; (7) Later editions of fiction with new illustrations, eight titles.

He lists the holdings of the ten leaders among the twenty-nine respondents.

Total titles held (maximum 130)

1.	British Museum	124
2.	Bodleian	117
3.	UCLA	110
4.	Private Collector	100
5.	University of Illinois	97
6.	Indiana University	96
7.	National Library of Scotland	89
8.	Yale University	87
9.	Harvard University	85
10.	Princeton University	82
	Average of twenty-nine respondents	56.8

Titles held in original condition (maximum 130)

1.	UCLA	100
2.	Private Collector	81
3.	Harvard University	74
4.	Indiana University	72
5.	Bodleian	70
6.	Princeton University	68
7.	British Museum	64
8.	Yale University	63
9.	New York Public Library	62
10.	University of Illinois	60
	Average of twenty-nine respondents	38.2

Dr. Ray remarks that among the six leading respondents with respect to titles held in original condition, one is a private collector and the holdings of three institutions derive mainly from the activities of private collectors--UCLA from Sadleir, Indiana from J.K. Lilly, and Princeton from Morris Parrish.

This is partly because of the fact that a considerable number of Dr. Ray's titles have appeared on such popular "100" lists as the Grolier's and A.E. Newton's, and the collectors, who eventually donated their libraries, naturally acquired such high spots. The libraries, if they acquired them by purchase at all, probably did so when they were issued (or if British, secured them as copyright deposits), and inevitably many were eventually rebound (*vide* the Bodleian and the British Museum.)

The comparative rarity, or lack of it, of some of the major works is interesting. Certainly this reviewer did not expect to see eighteen copies of Gissing's *Workers in the Dawn* (three volumes, London, 1891) recorded (only one rebound). And of minor works he certainly expected more than two copies of E.F. Benson's *Dodo: A Detail for the Day* (two volumes, London, 1893), to be reported, especially since he has a vivid memory of this work sitting on Scribner's shelves marked $6.50 for years. But then it was not on anyone's list.

Dr. Ray's findings emphasize the importance of the private collector in the preservation of many of these books. There is a high percentage of survival of high spots. However, in fields where private collecting was less popular, editions with textual revisions, new illustrations, magazine appearances, etc., the incidence of survival is startlingly low. And this is really an indictment of the librarians. This is the sort of food they should have been feeding their flocks, even if they couldn't afford the expensive firsts. But it seems they didn't. The fact appears to be that until very recent times most major libraries, certainly in England, were completely disinterested in the preservation (or at least the purchase) of modern literature in first editions.

Dr. Ray wisely points out that:

> As we pass from first editions to areas which have attracted far less attention, we shall find abundant illustration of the axiom that most of the printed materials which a scholar uses in his work are trash in the eyes of the collector. However, there is a compensating axiom that once the scholar has shown the importance of seemingly worthless material, the collector too becomes eager for it. And since we are clearly moving into an age of great scholarly editions, for which there will have to be assembled materials illustrating all stages of the development of each text from manuscript to final printed version, the emergence to visibility and consequent demand of books other than first editions can confidently be predicted.

Among the many interesting facts that come out of the statistics assembled here is that English librarians had (and probably still have) little interest in preserving or acquiring books issued "in parts." They did not acquire them when issued (and were not given them as copyright copies), and probably didn't regard them as books at all. It is startling to be told that the seven libraries reporting from England, Scotland, and Ireland have only one set in parts of *The Pickwick Papers*; between them The New York Public Library and Harvard have fifteen copies. And, incredibly, these libraries do not have, among them, a single copy of Lever's *Confessions of Harry Lorrequer*, Marryat's *Poor Jack*, Thackeray's *Vanity Fair*, or Surtees' *Mr. Sponge's Sporting Tour*, in parts.

The bibliographer of nineteenth-century Victorian fiction will of necessity have to depend on the resources of American libraries to supply, in original condition, the books he needs to examine.

The British have no one to blame but themselves for this really lamentable situation. The Michael Sadleir collection should never have left its shores, for one example. And they are now allowing to escape to America a vast quantity of modern manuscript material they will regret and resent in the future, the root reason being that except for a few souls they apparently don't believe such material is worth bothering to preserve.

Dr. Ray does not say much about the vexed problem of price, though he does comment that "if prices for rare books were in fact inflated in 1951, they are now swollen to the point of dropsy." This is quite true of much standard material. But why stick to that? His own list has thirty books in the classifications of "Later Editions. . . Important for Textual Corrections"; "Magazines in Which Fiction was First Serialized"; and "Later Editions . . . with New Illustrations." All thirty of these, if found, would cost less than a "Prime Pickwick in Parts"--only nobody has gone looking for them, at least until now.

It should be remembered that the passion for modern first editions is a comparatively recent phenomenon in the long history of book collecting and, at that, may not be a lasting one. Collectors and librarians may well take off in other directions, placing more emphasis on the later editions whose importance, and real rarity, Dr. Ray's census reveals.

24

Review of *Victorian Detective Fiction. A Catalogue of the Collection Made by Dorothy Glover & Graham Greene.* Bibliographically Arranged by Eric Osborne and Introduced by John Carter. With a Preface by Graham Greene. [From *The Book Collector*, 16 (Summer, 1967): 233-234, 237.]

THE Contents leaf of this attractively printed volume lists a brief *Preface* by Graham Greene, an engaging account of how it all began 'in the early days after the war.' There follows an admirable *Introduction* by John Carter; a *Compiler's Note* by Eric Osborne; the *Catalogue* itself, ending with number 471; an *Appendix* by Eric Sinclair Bell giving *The Publishing History of Fergus Hume's 'The Mystery of a Hansom Cab'; an Index of Detectives; Index of Illustrators; Index of Titles;* and *Colophon*, signed by Glover, Greene and Carter, but not by Osborne.

This is a curious smorgasbord. I have no ready definition for 'Victorian' but 55 of the titles included are by American authors and 54 are translations from French. The admirable exhibition of *Victorian Fiction* done for the National Book League some years ago by Carter and Sadleir admitted neither. Perhaps some such title as 'Detective Fiction Read by Victorians' would have been preferable. But even so, why include, for one example, Allan Pinkerton's *The Mollie Maguires and the Detective* (New York 1880), which is not only not its first edition, but is not even fiction. It only became fiction when Doyle cribbed extensively from it for his *Valley of Fear.* Only slightly over half of the titles are other than reprints, but perhaps this represents the current difficulty of obtaining these works in England in first editions.

This is an amateur's collection in *A New English Dictionary's* number 1 definition: 'One who loves or is fond *of.*' Miss Glover and Graham Greene qualify as its assembly obviously was a labour of love which engaged many happy hours searching, reading and eager discovery, an emotional experience which is fundamentally, the heart of the matter. It also qualifies, alas, to the *NED's* number 2 definition as: "Dabbler, or superficial student or worker'.

Why, one wonders, was it ever produced? Horace Walpole in the Preface to his *Description of Strawberry Hill* (1784), wrote: 'It will look, I fear, a little like arrogance in a private man to give a printed description of his collection'. Wilmarth Lewis comments that: 'he was speaking for all collectors who write about their collections. The collector is afraid of being thought arrogant if he publishes an account of his collection; but he has a still stronger fear, the fear that the world will not know that he has a collection worth writing about'. This collection was definitely either not worth writing about or was worth writing much more about. It lists author, title, publisher, brief collation, illustrator (if any), and 'Detective' with a very occasional comment. It is, in fact, a very sketchy check-list and frequently erroneous at that. Its errors begin, like the detective story itself, with Poe. His *Tales* is represented by a copy of the 'First London edition, 1846'. The correct date is 1845.

There are numerous other dating errors. That of the first English translation of DuBoisgobey's *The Golden Tress* is Philadelphia 1875, not 1879. Lynch's *The New Detective Story* is 'Chicago, Donnelley, Loyd & Co. 1882', not 'Chicago, Henry A. Summer & Co. 1884', while 'Waters' *The Experiences of a French Detective Officer*, in the undated Charles H. Clarke edition, is only possibly (1861). Sadleir, a more reliable guide, lists it as '1st Edition, n.d.?' And surely the anonymous *A Strange Case* 'Excerpted from *Tinsley's Magazine*' could have been more accurately dated than '*c*. 1870' without too much arduous research.

A certain class-consciousness seems to enter into Miss Dorothy Glover's identification of detectives. In B.L. Farjeon's *Samuel Boyd of Catchpole Square* she lists 'Inspector Robinson, Scotland Yard,' and in Lawrence Lynch's *The Unseen Hand*, 'Inspector Haines, Chicago Police' as detectives. The detectives who did the actual detecting in these cases were not such grand persons as 'Inspectors'; they were David Lambert and Robert Jocelyn, detectives. In Dick Donovan's *The Man from Manchester* and *Tracked to Doom* the detective was not Donovan, but rather, respectively, Farabin Tindal and Colvin Sugg. In the very last entry, Edmund Yates' *A Silent Witness*, the detective was not 'Clement Burton, M.D.' but Sergeant Francis, Scotland Yard. And surely in the *Index of Detectives* which has a category 'Female

Detectives', mention might have been made of the very first, in Wilkie Collins's *No Name*. She shall remain unnamed here: those curious should read the book. She was not very successful.

It also seems a shame, with such material at hand, that the occasional notes were not elaborated. A fascinating edition of Poe's *Tales of Mystery, Imagination & Humour; and Poems*, (Vizetelly 1852), is listed:

> 'Reprint, pp (xxiv), 256, half calf.
> Illustrator: anonymous woodcuts.
> *Detective*: Dupin
> This edition not in the British Museum.'

This is all we are told and it is not enough. It is perhaps unfair to task the compilers of what is after all the briefest sort of check-list with not producing a full dress bibliography but surely when an elaborate *Appendix* lists the publishing history of 'The Mystery of Hansom Cab' down to 1959, something more should be said about this than 'Reprint'.

It is a very important book with an interesting history. It is the first volume of Vizetelly's famous 'Readable Books' series and was originally published in Penny Weekly Numbers, not a one of which is now known. It is the first illustrated edition of Poe, the first to be printed in England, (the 1845 *Tales* were imported sheets) and is a great rarity: published in boards and cloth, no copy of the latter binding is recorded.

Poe's famed *The Gold Bug* is here entitled *The Gold-Beetle*, in deference to contemporary British mores.

Anyone with a modicum of curiosity about these matters should consult Scribner's catalogue 98, *Detective Fiction. A Collection of First and a few early Editions*, (New York 1934), John Carter's pioneer compilation. The last copy I saw offered was priced $1.50. It is not copyrighted and some enterprising publisher could surely profitably reproduce it to sell for considerably less than £5 5s, net.

PART III

CHRONOLOGICAL CHECKLIST
OF THE WRITINGS OF
DAVID A. RANDALL

The published writings of David A. Randall are listed here in chronological order by year of publication. Within each year, books, exhibition catalogues, and articles are listed alphabetically by title, followed by book reviews which are arranged alphabetically by the title of the book reviewed, and then by letters to the editor arranged alphabetically by the name of the publication in which the letter appears when no title has been assigned to the letter and then alphabetically by title for those letters which have been assigned a title.

A number of entries are preceded by ellipses. These indicate a generic heading, such as "bibliographical note" or "query." All contributions to continuing columns or a series of articles are entered under the date of the first publication of the column or series. Mr. Randall reprinted several of his earlier articles, usually revised, in *Dukedom Large Enough*. Other reprints are cited with the entry for the original work. Reviews of writings by Mr. Randall are listed alphabetically by the title of the journal in which the review is found and are included in the entry for the work reviewed. Randall served as department editor for several journals during his career and these editorships are cited first in the list of writings for the year in which the work began.

One of the glories of The Lilly Library is the series of exhibition catalogues which David Randall established. His influence is pervasive in all of those issued during his tenure (1956-1975) and we have listed here those which can be determined to have been contributed to directly by him.

Important collections of correspondence, notes, publications, memorabilia and other material relating to David A.

Randall are located at The Lilly Library, Indiana University, Bloomington, and in the private collection of Ronald R. Randall in Santa Barbara, California.

CHRONOLOGICAL CHECKLIST

1930   [Review] *English Collectors of of Books and Manuscripts (1530-1930)* by Seymour De Ricci. *Publishers' Weekly*, 118 (November 15): 2293.

1931   "The Legion of the Lost," *The Colophon, A Book Collectors' Quarterly*, 7 (September): [5-12].

[Review] *American First Editions and Their Prices* by William Targ; *1100 Obscure Points* by Jacob Schwartz; *A Catalogue of the Altschul Collection of George Meredith in the Yale University Library* comp. by Bertha Coolidge. *Publishers' Weekly*, 119 (June 20): 2886-2889.

[Review] *Collecting American First Editions--Its Pitfalls and Pleasures* by Richard Curle. *Publishers' Weekly*, 119 (February 21): 973-975. With Michael Papantonio.

[Review] *Fishers of Books* by Barton Currie. *Publishers' Weekly*, 120 (September 19): 1272-1273.

1932   [Review] *Annals of an Era, Percy Mackaye and the Mackaye Family, 1826-1932* by Edwin O. Grover; *Booth Tarkington, A Bibliography* by Barton Currie. *Publishers' Weekly*, 122 (October 15): 1525-1526.

[Review] *The First Editions of Henry William Herbert, "Frank Forester," 1807-1858. A Checklist* comp. by Paul S. Seybolt. *Publishers' Weekly*, 122 (September 24): 1276.

[Review] *The First Editions of the Writings of Charles Dickens, Their Points and Values*, rev. and enlarged ed. by John C. Eckel. *Publishers' Weekly*, 122 (September 17): 1051-1053.

[Review] *A Handbook of the Literature of the Rev. C. L. Dodgson (Lewis Carroll)* by Sidney Williams and Falconer Maden. *Publishers' Weekly*, 121 (February 20): 868-869.

[Review] *Modern English First Editions and Their Prices* by William Targ. *Publishers' Weekly*, 121 (April 16): 1741-1742, 1744.

[Review] *Selective Bibliography of American Literature 1775-1900* by B. W. Fullerton; *A Census of First Editions and Source Materials by Edgar Allan Poe in American Collections* comp. by Charles F. Heartman and Kenneth Rede. *Publishers' Weekly*, 122 (November 19): 1940-1942.

1933   [Review] *A Bibliography of the Writings of Edith Wharton* by Lavinia Davis. *Publishers' Weekly*, 123 (June 17): 1975-1976.

[Review] *Frank Forester (Henry William Herbert), A Tragedy in Exile* by William Southworth Hunt. *Publishers' Weekly*, 124 (July 1): 29-30.

[Review] *Louisa May Alcott, A Bibliography* by Lucile Gulliver; *Sinclair Lewis, A Biographical Sketch* by Carl Van Doren with a Bibliography by Harvey Taylor. *Publishers' Weekly*, 123 (January 21): 242-243.

1934   "American First Editions 1900-1933," in *New Paths in Book Collecting; Essays by Various Hands*, ed. by John Carter. London: Constable, pp. 193-219. Reprinted Freeport, New York: Books for Libraries, 1967. Reprinted as a separate as *Collecting American First Editions, 1900-1933*. New York: Scribners, n.d.

[Review] *Bibliography of the Writings of Edgar A. Poe* by John W. Robertson. *Publishers' Weekly*, 125 (April 21): 1540-1543.

[Review] *An Enquiry into the Nature of Certain Nineteenth Century Pamphlets* by John Carter and Graham Pollard. *Publishers' Weekly*, 126 (July 7): 54-56.

1935   Editor (American). *Bibliographical Notes and Queries,*
    October, 1935-May, 1939.

. . . "Linotype Printing . . . *The Tribune Book of Open-Air
Sports,*" *Bibliographical Notes and Queries,* 1
(April): 2.

. . . "Mrs. Browning's *Sonnets from the Portuguese,*"
Bibliographical Notes and Queries, 1 (August): 2.

. . . "Tennyson's *Maud,*" *Bibliographical Notes and
Queries,* 1 (August): 1.

. . . "Washington Irving: *Salmagundi,*" *Bibliographical
Notes and Queries,* 1 (April): 11.

"Waverly in America," *The Colophon, A Quarterly for
Bookmen,* New Series, 1 (Summer): 39-55.

1936   . . . "Ainsworth: *Nell Gwyn* (1850)," *Bibliographical Notes
and Queries,* 2 (April): 6.

. . . "Alcott, Louisa May: *Moods,*" *Bibliographical Notes
and Queries,* 2 (May): 6.

. . . "Alcott: *The Mysterious Key and What It Opened*
(Boston, 1867)," *Bibliographical Notes and Queries,*
2 (April): 6.

. . . "Aldrich: *The Story of a Bad Boy,*" *Bibliographical
Notes and Queries,* 2 (April): 3.

. . . "American Arithmetics," *Bibliographical Notes and
Queries,* 2 (April): 7.

. . . "Conrad: *Some Reminiscences* (1908)," *Bibliographical Notes and Queries,* 2 (May): 9.

[Contribution] "The Crow's Nest," *The Colophon, A
Quarterly for Bookmen,* New Series, 1 (Winter):
469, 471.

. . . "Emmett, Dan: *Dixie,*" *Bibliographical Notes and
Queries,* 2 (May): 10.

. . . "Frank Forester: *Supplement to Fish and Fishing,*"
Bibliographical Notes and Queries, 2 (April): 7.

. . . "Grossmith: *The Diary of a Nobody,*" *Bibliographical
Notes and Queries,* 2 (May): 10.

*Henry William Herbert (Frank Forester): A Bibliography of
His Writings 1832-1858.* Compiled by William
Mitchell Van Winkle with the Bibliographical

The Southworth-Anthoensen Press. Reprinted New York: Burt Franklin, 1971.

Review:

> *New York Times Book Review,* (August 2, 1936): 18.

. . . "Jonathan Edwards," *Bibliographical Notes and Queries,* 2 (April): 5.

. . . "Karl Marx: *Das Kapital,*" *Bibliographical Notes and Queries,* 2 (May): 10.

"Kipling and Collecting," *Publishers' Weekly,* 129 (January 25): 379-380.

. . . "Marryat: *Valerie* (1849)," *Bibliographical Notes and Queries,* 2 (April): 7.

. . . "Millay: *Renascence* (First Separate Edition)," *Bibliographical Notes and Queries,* 2 (May): 11.

. . . "*Swing Low, Sweet Chariot,*" *Bibliographical Notes and Queries,* 2 (May): 12.

. . . "Wallace: *Ben Hur,*" *Bibliographical Notes and Queries,* 2 (May): 12.

[Review] *Merle Johnson's American First Editions,* 3rd ed., rev. by Jacob Blanck. *Publishers' Weekly,* 130 (November 28): 2108-2109.

1937 . . . "Webb, S. and B.: *Soviet Communism,*" *Bibliographical Notes and Queries,* 2 (February): 4.

1938 "Footnote on a Minor Poet," *The Colophon, A Quarterly for Bookmen,* New Series, 3 (Autumn): 587-597.

1939 "One Hundred Good Novels," *Publishers' Weekly,* 135 (May 20): 1851-1853, ["*The Story of a Bad Boy*"]; (June 17): 2183-2184, "*Little Women*"; 136 (July 15): 180-182, "Henry Adams: *Democracy*"; (August 19): 541-543, "[Hawkins, Anthony Hope] 'Anthony Hope' *The Prisoner of Zenda*"; (October 21): 1625-1626, "Crane, Stephen: *The Red Badge of Courage*"; (November 25): 1985-1986, "Harte, Bret, *The Luck of Roaring Camp*"; 137 (January 20, 1940): 255-257, "Melville, Herman: *Moby Dick,*" "Melville, Herman" *The Whale*"; (March 16): 1181-1182,

"Hawthorne, Nathaniel: *The Scarlet Letter*"; (April 27): 1688-1689, "Ford, Paul Leicester: *The Honorable Peter Stirling*"; (May 18): 1931-1933, "Stowe, Harriet Beecher: *Uncle Tom's Cabin*"; 138 (July 20): 191-192, "Wharton, Edith: *Ethan Frome*"; (August 17): 491-494, "Richardson, Samuel: *Pamela*"; (September 21): 1173-1175, "Dana, Richard Henry: *Two Years Before the Mast*"; 139 (January 18, 1941): 268-269, "[Bronte, Charlotte]: *Jane Eyre*"; (February 15): 860-862, "Wallace, Lew: *Ben-Hur*"; (May 17): 2031-2032, "Austen, Jane: *Emma*"; 140 (July 19): 186-187, "James, Henry: *The Portrait of a Lady*"; (August 16): 486-487, "Taylor, Bayard: *The Story of Kennett*"; (October 18): 1590-1591, "Harris, Joel Chandler: *Uncle Remus*"; (November 15): 1926-1927, "Atherton, Gertrude: *The Conqueror*"; 141 (January 17, 1942): 209-210, "Bennett, Arnold: *The Old Wives' Tale*"; (February 21): 898-899, "Galsworthy, John: *The Man of Property*"; (March 21): 1200-1202, "Fielding, Henry: *The History of Tom Jones.*" Collations by David A. Randall, Notes by John T. Winterich.

1940   Editor (with others) "Bibliographical Notes," *Papers of the Bibliographical Society of America*, 1940-1941.

. . . "Doyle, A. Conan (1879-1928). *Memoirs of Sherlock Holmes* . . . ," *Papers of the Bibliographical Society of America*, 34 (Second Quarter): 190-191.

. . . "Lever, Charles (1806-1872). *Our Mess* . . . ," *Papers of the Bibliographical Society of America*, 34 (Third Quarter): 274-276.

. . . "Thackeray, W. M. (1811-1863). *Vanity Fair* . . . ," *Papers of the Bibliographical Society of America*, 34 (Second Quarter): 191-192.

. . . "Thackeray, William Makepeace (1811-1863). *Vanity Fair* . . . ," *Papers of the Bibliographical Society of America*, 34 (Third Quarter): 276-278.

[Review] *A Bibliography of the First Printings of the Writings of Edgar Allan Poe* comp. by Charles F.

Heartman and James R. Canny. *Publishers' Weekly*, 138 (November 30): 2033-2038.

1941   [Review] *Wilkie Collins and Charles Reade. First Editions (with a few exceptions) in the Library at Dormy House, Pine Valley, New Jersey* by M. L. Parrish. *Papers of the Bibliographical Society of America*, 35 (Second Quarter): 168-171.

1942   . . . "Brooke, Rupert (1887-1915). *The Collected Poems*. . . ," *Papers of the Bibliographical Society of America*, 36 (First Quarter): 68.
. . . "Grey, Zane (1872-1930). *Riders of the Purple Sage*. . .," *Papers of the Bibliographical Society of America*, 36 (First Quarter): 68.
[Obituary of Max Harzof] *Publishers' Weekly*, 141 (January 10): 123-124.
[Review] *A Bibliography of the Strawberry Hill Press with a Record of the Prices at Which Copies Have Been Sold* by A. T. Hazen. *Publishers' Weekly*, 142 (August 15): 484-486.

1944   "The Adventures of Two Bibliophiles," *New York Times Book Review*, (August 6): 14, 16.
"The Hogan Sale of American Literature," *Publishers' Weekly*, 146 (November 25): 2068-2070.
"The New Bibliography of American Literature," *Library Journal*, 69 (June 15): 549-550. With Carroll A. Wilson, James T. Babb, Clarence S. Brigham, and William A. Jackson.
[Review] *Letters of Thomas J. Wise to John Henry Wrenn* ed. by Fannie E. Ratchford. *New York Times Book Reivew*, (December 17): 3, 14, 16.

1946   Editor, "Bibliographical Notes," *The Baker Street Journal*, January, 1946-October, 1947.
"The Adventure of the Notorious Forger," *The Baker Street Journal*, 1 (July): 371-377. Reprinted San Francisco: Randall & Windle, 1978.
"The Battle of Books, Or the Auction is the Payoff,"

Publishers' Weekly, 149 (May 11): 2576-2577.
"A Census of the Known Existing Original Manuscripts of the Sacred Writings," *The Baker Street Journal*, 1 (October): 504-508.
"Charles Dickens and Richard Bently," *Times Literary Supplement*, (October 12): 496.
"George Washington, Father of His Country and Governor Posey?," *The Indiana Quarterly for Bookmen*, 2 (October): 122-128.
"A Plea for a More Consistent Policy of Cataloguing by Auction Galleries," *Papers of the Bibliographical Society of America*, 40 (Second Quarter): 107-126.
A Primer of Book-Collecting. By John T. Winterich in Collaboration with David A. Randall. Newly Revised and Enlarged Edition. New York: Greenberg Publisher.
Reviews:
> *Booklist*, 43 (February 15, 1947): 190.
> *Chicago Sun Book Weekly*, (February 2, 1947): 5.
> *San Francisco Chronicle*, (November 11, 1946): 16.
> *Times Literary Supplement*, (May 24, 1947): 260.

"A Study of *A Study in Scarlet*, London: Ward Lock & Co., 1888; or, A Scandal in Bibliography," *The Baker Street Journal*, 1 (January): 103-106.
"*The Valley of Fear* Bibliographically Considered," *The Baker Street Journal*, 1 (April): 232-237.
[Review] *Between the Lines: Letters and Memoranda Exchanged Between H. Buxton Forman and Thomas J. Wise* with a Foreword by Carl H. Pforzheimer and an Introductory Essay and Notes by Fannie E. Ratchford. *Publishers' Weekly*, 149 (June 8): 3054-3056.

1947   "Bibliographical Notes," *The Baker Street Journal*, 2 (January): 104-105.
"A Tentative Enquiry into the Earliest Printings, In Book Form, of the First Four Sherlock Holmes Short

Stories: A Scandal in Bohemia, The Red-Headed
League, A Case of Identity and the Boscombe
Valley Mystery; With a Conclusion Tending to Prove
That In the Case of Two of Them Certainly, and Two
of Them Possibly--America First!," *The Baker Street
Journal*, 2 (October): 491-496.
[Reviews] *Carrousel for Bibliophiles* ed. by William Targ;
Invitation to Book Collecting by Colton Storm and
Howard Peckham; *One Hundred Influential
American Books Printed before 1900* ed. by
Frederick B. Adams, Jr.; *A Catalogue of the First
Editions of First Books in the Collection of Paul S.
Seybolt. New York Times Book Review*, (April 13): 4.

1948   "The Court of Appeals," *The New Colophon*, 1 (January):
81-85; (April): 190-197; (July): 291-295; (October):
401-407; 2 (January, 1949): 82-88, 90-93; (June):
172-176; (September: 277-285; (February, 1950):
379-383.
"Notes Towards a Correct Collation of the First Edition of
Vanity Fair," *Papers of the Bibliographical Society of
America*, 42 (Second Quarter): 95-109.

1950   *Thirteen Author Collections of the Nineteenth Century and
Five Centuries of Familiar Quotations.* By Carroll A.
Wilson. Ed. by Jean C. S. Wilson and David A.
Randall. New York: Privately Printed for Charles
Scribners's Sons.

1951   [Review] *A Stevenson Library. Catalogue of a Collection
of Writings By and About Robert Louis Stevenson,
Formed by Edwin J. Beinecke*, volume one, comp.
by George L. McKay. *Papers of the Bibliographical
Society of America*, 45 (Third Quarter): 268-270.

1953   "Book-Collecting As a Hobby," *Antiquarian Bookman*, 11
(April 11): 1283-1285.
"The Sadleir Collection," in *The Sadleir Collection:
Addresses Delivered by Frederick B. Adams, Jr, and
David A. Randall at the Dedication Ceremonies,*

*University of California at Los Angeles Library,
November 13, 1952.* Los Angeles: Friends of the
UCLA Library, pp. 13-19.

1955   [Review] *Beatrix Potter: A Bibliographic Check List* by
       Jane Quinby. *Papers of the Bibliographic Society of
       America*, 49 (Fourth Quarter): 375-376.

1956   *A Brief and true relation of some small portion of Books &
       MSS. comprising part of the renowned library of J.
       K. Lilly, Eagle Crest, Indianapolis and now by his
       benefaction situated at Indiana University, Hastily
       and   inadequately   compiled   for   the
       bibliocognoscenti of Ye Caxton Club, Chicago,
       Northwest Terr. By Prof. David A. Randall, servant of
       the above named, Oct. 2, 1956.* [Bloomington:
       Indiana University].
       "Institutional Collecting of Books and Manuscripts," in
       *Proceedings of the Conference on Materials for
       Research in American Culture, October 25-27, 1956,
       The University of Texas.* Austin: The University of
       Texas, pp. 13-19.

1957   "Josiah Kirby Lilly," *The Book Collector*, 6 (Autumn): 263-
       277. (Contemporary Collectors XIV).
       "Report of the Rare Book Librarian, July, 1956-June, 1957,"
       The Indiana University Bookman, No. 2
       (November): 38-47.

1958   "A Backward Glance Over Travel'd Roads," *The Indiana
       University Bookman*, No. 3 (December): 3-79.
       *An Exhibition from the Indiana University Library of
       Original Printings of Some Milestones in Medical
       History and Natural Science, Aristotle (1476) to Salk
       (1951) With Emphasis on Biology--Botany (Largely
       from the J. K. Lilly collection) On the Occasion of
       the Annual Meeting of the American Institute of
       Biological Sciences, August 24-28, 1958, Indiana
       University.* Bloomington: Indiana University
       Library.

Report of the Rare Book Librarian, Indiana University, July 1957-June 1958. Bloomington: Indiana University Library.

[Letter] "Authors' Manuscripts," *Times Literary Supplement,* (November 7): 641.

1959   "Frank J. Hogan, 1877-1944," in *Grolier 75: A Biographical Retrospective to Celebrate the Seventy-fifth Anniversary of The Grolier Club in New York.* New York: The Grolier Club, pp. 200-202.

Report of the Rare Book Librarian, Indiana University, July 1958-June 1959. Bloomington: Indiana University Library.

1960   *Dedication of The Lilly Library, Indiana University, October 3, 1960.* Bloomington: Indiana University, The Lilly Library.

. . . "The First American Edition of the Brontes' *Poems,*" *The Book Collector,* 9 (Summer): 199-201.

. . . "Housman Manuscripts," *The Book Collector,* 9 (Winter): 456.

"The J. K. Lilly Collection of Edgar Allan Poe," *The Indiana University Bookman,* No. 4 (March): 46-58.

"The New Testament Portion of the First Edition of the Bible and the First Book Printed with Moveable Types." Broadside. [Bloomington: Indiana University, The Lilly Library].

. . . "*A Shropshire Lad* with a Variant Title-Page," *The Book Collector,* 9 (Winter): 458-459.

"Two States of 'Two Lives,'" *Papers of the Bibliographical Society of America,* 54 (Fourth Quarter): 295.

1961   *A. E. Housman: A Collection of Manuscripts, Letters, Proofs, First Editions, Etc. Formed by H. B. Collamore of West Hartford, Connecticut, Presented to The Lilly Library, Indiana University.* Bloomington: Indiana University, The Lilly Library.

"Bruce Rogers' First Decorated Book," *Papers of the Bibliographical Society of America,* 55 (First Quarter): 40-42.

... "A Dedication Grolier Discovered Recovered," *The Book Collector*, 10 (Spring): 66-68.

"How We Found the Manuscript," *Publishers' Weekly*, 179 (June 19): 37-39. With Percy Muir. Reprinted in *Memoirs of James II, His Campaigns as Duke of York 1652-1660*, Bloomington: Indiana University Press, 1962, pp. 13-23.

Review:

  Saturday Review, 45 (March 31, 1962): 18.

"Mr Muir and Gabriel Wells: A Rejoinder," *The Book Collector*, 10 (Spring): 53-55. Reprinted in *Antiquarian Bookman*, 27 (May 15, 1961): 1902.

Report of the Rare Book Librarian, The Lilly Library, Indiana University, July 1959-June 1961. Bloomington: Indiana University Library.

[Letter] *Antiquarian Bookman*, 27 (March 13): 964.

[Letter] "Moderns in the Auction Room," *Times Literary Supplement*, (August 11): 515. Quoted in *Antiquarian Bookman*, 28 (October 16, 1961): 1358.

1962   "'Dukedom Large Enough' I. Changing the Gutenberg Census," *Papers of the Bibliographical Society of America*, 56 (Second Quarter): 157-174.

"'Dukedom Large Enough' II. Hemingway, Churchill, and the Printed Word," *Papers of the Bibliographical Society of America*, 56 (Third Quarter): 346-353.

"'Dukedom Large Enough' III. Thomas Jefferson and The Declaration of Independence," *Papers of the Bibliographical Society of America*, 56 (Fourth Quarter): 472-480.

1963   "'Dukedom Large Enough' IV. The Permanent Questionnaire," *Papers of the Bibliographical Society of America*, 57 (First Quarter): 68-76.

Exhibition of Original Printings of Some Milestones of Science from Pliny (1469) to Banting (1922). Bloomington: Indiana University, The Lilly Library.

Grolier: or 'Tis Sixty Years Since. A Reconstruction of the Exhibit of 100 Books Famous in English Literature Originally Held in New York, 1903, on the Occasion

of the Club's Visit to The Lilly Library, Indiana University, May 1, 1963. Bloomington: Indiana University, The Lilly Library.
Review:
Times Literary Supplement, (October 11, 1963): 816
"IPEX," *Antiquarian Bookman,* 32 (September 30): 1199-1201.
Report of the Rare Book Librarian, The Lilly Library, Indiana University, July 1, 1961-June 30, 1963. Bloomington: Indiana University, The Lilly Library.

1964 "Check List: Andrew Lang Fairy Books," *Antiquarian Bookman,* 34 (August 31): 805.
. . . "The First American Edition of *1914 and Other Poems,*" *The Book Collector,* 13 (Autumn): 359.
The J. K. Lilly Collection of Edgar Allan Poe: An Account of Its Formation. Bloomington: Indiana University, The Lilly Library.
Manuscripts Ancient-Modern: An Exhibition on the Occasion of the Manuscript Society's Annual Meeting. Held at the Lilly Library, Indiana University, October 1-4, 1964. Bloomington: Indiana University, The Lilly Library.
Review:
Times Literary Supplement, (January 7, 1965): 16.
[Letter] *Antiquarian Bookman,* 34 (September 21): 1045.
[Letter] "John Addington Symonds," *Times Literary Supplement,* (December 31): 1181.
[Letter] "More Copies Than One," *Times Literary Supplement,* (April 23): 343.
[Letter] "Peter Pan," *Times Literary Supplement,* (January 9): 34.

1965 "Gilbert and Sullivan's 'Princess Ida,'" *Papers of the Bibliographical Society of America,* 59 (Third Quarter): 322-326.
"The Gondoliers," *Papers of the Bibliographical Society of America,* 59 (Second Quarter): 193-198.

Report of the Rare Book Librarian, The Lilly Library,
Indiana University, July 1, 1963-June 30, 1965.
Bloomington: Indiana University, The Lilly Library.
Three Centuries of American Poetry: An Exhibition of
Original Printings. Bloomington: Indiana University,
The Lilly Library.
[Review] *Bibliographical Resources for the Study of*
Nineteenth Century English Fiction by Gordon N.
Ray. *Papers of the Bibliographical Society of*
America, 59 (Second Quarter): 208-211.
[Letter] "The Irish Mafia," *Times Literary Supplement,*
(February 25): 156.

1966   . . . "Copies of Conrad's *Chance,* Dated '1913,'" *The Book*
Collector, 15 (Spring): 68.
Eighty-Nine Good Novels of the Sea, the Ship, and the
Sailor. A List Compiled by J. K. Lilly. An Account of
Its Formation. Bloomington: Indiana University,
The Lilly Library.
"J. K. Lilly: America's Quiet Collector," *Antiquarian*
Bookman, 37 (June 27): 2679-2681. Reprinted
[Indianapolis, 1966?]; *Indianapolis Star Magazine,*
(April 2, 1967): 20, 22, 24; *Oregon GP,* 15 (August,
1966): 8-9, 21; *Report of the Rare Book Librarian,*
The Lilly Library, Indiana University, July 1, 1965-
June 30, 1967. Bloomington: Indiana University,
The Lilly Library, 1967, pp. 1-7.
The John Carter Collection of A.E. Housman.
Bloomington: Indiana University, The Lilly Library.
Medicine: An Exhibition of Books Relating to Medicine
and Surgery from the Collection formed by J.K. Lilly.
Bloomington: Indiana University, The Lilly Library.
A Primer of Book Collecting. Third Rev. Ed. New York:
Crown Publishers. New York: Bell Publishing
Company. London: G. Allen & Unwin, Ltd. With
John T. Winterich.
Reviews:
          Library Association Record, 70 (January,
          1968):25.

Saturday Review, 49 (October 22, 1966): 59-60.

Times Literary Supplement, (September 28, 1967):924.

[Letter] *Antiquarian Bookman*, 38 (October 3): 1294.

[Letter] *Antiquarian Bookman*, 38 (November 21-28): 20-27.

[Letter] "Economics of Book Collecting," *Times Literary Supplement*, (January 27): 63.

1967   *The First Twenty-five Years of Printing, 1455-1480: An Exhibition.* Bloomington: Indiana University, The Lilly Library.

[Review] *Records of a Bibliographer: Selected Papers of William Alexander Jackson*, ed. and introduced by William H. Bond. *Library Journal*, 92 (September 15): 3018.

[Review] *Victorian Detective Fiction: A Catalogue of the Collection Made by Dorothy Glover & Graham Greene* Bibliographically Arranged by Eric Osborne and Introduced by John Carter with a Preface by Graham Greene. *The Book Collector*, 16 (Summer): 233-234, 237.

[Letter] *AB Bookman's Weekly*, 39 (June 5-12): 2316.

[Letter] *Times Literary Supplement*, (March 9): 202.

[Letter] "Garland for Gutenberg," *Times Literary Supplement*, (July 27): 694.

1968   *American Patriotic Songs: Yankee Doodle to The Conquered Banner, with Emphasis on The Star Spangled Banner. An Exhibition held at The Lilly Library, Indiana University, Bloomington, July-September, 1968.* Bloomington: Indiana University, The Lilly Library.

Five Centuries of Familiar Quotations in Their Earliest Appearances in Print: September 1, 1968 - January 1, 1969. Bloomington: Indiana University, The Lilly Library.

"Sherlock, Tobacco, and a Gold-Headed Cane," in *The Last Bookman: A Journey into the Life & Times of*

Vincent Starrett (Author-Journalist-Bibliophile). By
Peter Ruber. New York: The Candlelight Press,
Inc., pp. 77-79.

1969   "AB Quotes" [From *Dukedom Large Enough*], *AB
Bookman's Weekly*, 44 (September 15): 758, 762,
764.
"Booksellers and Collectors: A Dealer's Apprenticeship,"
Publishers' Weekly, 196 (July 21): 35-38.
Dukedom Large Enough. New York: Random House.
Reviews:
> *AB Bookman's Weekly*, 44 (September 15,
> 1969): 755, 758.
> *Alameda* (California) *Times-Star*, (November
> 20, 1969): 1.
> *Chicago Daily News "Panorama,"* (December
> 6-7, 1969): 6.
> *The Hominy* (Oklahoma) *News*, (October 16,
> 1969).
> King Features Syndicate column by Mel
> Heimer, September 25, 1969.
> *Kirkus Reviews,* 37 (May 15, 1969): 592-593.
> *Journal of Library History*, 6 (January, 1971):
> 91-93.
> *Library Journal*, 94 (September 15, 1969):
> 3030-3031.
> *New York Times Book Review*, (August 31,
> 1969): 4.
> *Publishers' Weekly*, 195 (May 12, 1969): 55.
> *San Francisco Chronicle*, (August 27, 1969):
> 33.
> *Saturday Review*, 52 (September 6, 1969):
> 33.

*An Exhibit of Seventeenth-Century Editions of Writings by
John Milton.* Bloomington: Indiana University, The
Lilly Library.
Review:
> *Times Literary Supplement*, (March 13, 1969):
> 277.

An *Exhibit of Seventeenth-Century Editions of Writings by John Milton in Memory of William Riley Parker, 1906-1968, Distinguished Professor of English, Indiana University, Author of "Milton: A Biography," Oxford at the Clarendon Press, 1968.* Bloomington: Indiana University, The Lilly Library.

Report of the Rare Book Librarian, The Lilly Library, Indiana University, July 1, 1967-June 30, 1969. Bloomington: Indiana University, The Lilly Library.

[Letter] *AB Bookman's Weekly,* 43 (April 28): 1606.

[Letter] *AB Bookman's Weekly,* 43 (August 4-11): 313.

1970 *The Beginnings of Higher Education in Indiana: An Exhibit Commemorating the Sesquicentennial of Indiana University.* Bloomington: Indiana University, The Lilly Library.

Biology. An Exhibition at the Lilly Library in Honor of the Meetings of The American Institute of Biological Sciences and The American Psychological Society. Bloomington: Indiana University, The Lilly Library.

An *Exhibition of Books from the Firm of Lathrop C. Harper, Inc., Presented to the Lilly Library by Mrs. Bernardo Mendel.* Bloomington: Indiana University, The Lilly Library.

The Ian Fleming Collection of 19th-20th Century Source Material Concerning Western Civilization together with the Originals of the James Bond-007 Tales. Bloomington: Indiana University, The Lilly Library.
Review:
> *Times Literary Supplement,* (July 23, 1971): 868.

[Letter] "'The Wrong Box'," *Times Literary Supplement,* (November 13): 1328.

1971 *An Exhibition on the Occasion of the Transfer of Public Papers of the Honorable Joseph W. Barr to the Lilly Library, Indiana University.* Bloomington: Indiana University, The Lilly Library.

1972   . . . "Ian Fleming's First Book," *The Book Collector*, 21
(Autumn): 414-415.

1973   *An Exhibition of American Literature Honoring the
Completion of the Editorial Work on the 100th
Volume Approved by the Center for Editions of
American Authors, together with Eighteenth-Century
American Fiction Published Abroad, Eighteenth-
Century American Editions of Some English Fiction,
Eighteenth-Century American Drama, The First
Quarter Century of Fiction Written and Published in
America: 1774-1799.* Bloomington: Indiana
University, The Lilly Library.
*The First Hundred Years of Detective Fiction, 1841-1941,
by One Hundred Authors on the Hundred Thirtieth
Anniversary of the First Publicaztion in Book Form
of Edgar Allan Poe's "The Murder in the Rue
Morgue" Philadelphia, 1843. An Exhibition Held at
The Lilly Library, Indiana University, Bloomington,
July-September, 1973.* Bloomington: Indiana
University, The Lilly Library.
Review:
Times Literary Supplement, September 14,
1973): 1064.
Printing and the Mind of Man. Bloomington: Indiana
University, The Lilly Library.
"*A Shropshire Lad* Label Variants," *The Book Collector*, 22
(Summer): 176.
[Review] *The Collector's Book of Detective Fiction* by Eric
Quale. *The Book Collector*, 22 (Summer): 246, 249.

1974   *An Exhibition Honoring the Seventy-Fifth Birthday of
Hoagland Howard Carmichael, L.L. B., 1926, D.M.,
1972, Indiana University.* Bloomington: Indiana
University, The Lilly Library.
*Science Fiction/Fantasy: An Exhibition of Books Relating
to Science Fiction and Fantasy from the Lilly
Collection.* Bloomington: Indiana University, The
Lilly Library.

[Tribute to Percy H. Muir] in *P.H.M. 80. 17 December 1974.* n.p., s.n., pp. 18-20.

1975   *Science Fiction and Fantasy: An Exhibition.* Bloomington: Indiana University, The Lilly Library.

PART IV

CHECKLIST OF WRITINGS ABOUT DAVID A. RANDALL

1935   "Randall Joins Scribner Staff," *Publishers' Weekly,* 127 (March 16): 1172.

1938   Clampitt, Helen. *Lines Written After Reading "The Bibliography of Henry William Herbert" Compiled by Wm. Mitchell Van Winkle and David A. Randall.* n.p.: Henderson Hay is typewritten at the end.
      Strakosch, Avery, "David Randall of Scribner's," *Avocations, A Magazine of Hobbies and Leisure,* 2 (April): 53-56.

1952   Martin, Pete, "He Finds Fortunes in Forgotten Corners," *The Saturday Evening Post,* 224 (March 22): 42-43, 111-112, 114-116, 118.

1956   "Personnel, David A. Randall," *College and Research Libraries,* 17 (May): 259.

1959   "Indiana's Bookman," *Time,* 73 (April 13): 54, 57.

1969   Randall, David A. *Dukedom Large Enough.* New York: Random House. Caption title: "Reminiscences of a Rare Book Dealer, 1929-1956."

1975   "David A. Randall" by William R. Cagle in *To Honor Retiring Faculty, Indiana University, April 22, 1975* [Bloomington: Indiana University, p. 15].

The David A. Randall Retrospective Memorial Exhibition: Twenty Years' Acquisitions. The Exhibits chosen by Mr. Randall and described by Josiah Q. Bennett. Bloomington: Indiana University Library, The Lilly Library.

1980   Rostenberg, Leona and Madeleine B. Stern, "Antiquarian Booksellers and Their Memoirs," *AB Bookman's Weekly*, 66 (December 22-29): 4186, 4190, 4192, 4194, 4196, 4198-4206.

1982   Adelman, Seymour. *Help from Heaven.* New Castle, Delaware: Oak Knoll Books.

1986   Randall, David V. "A Literary Friendship," *Pennsylvania Portfolio*, 4 (Fall/Winter, 1986/87): 16-17.

Obituaries

1975   Chernofsky, Jacob L., "Obituary Notes, David A. Randall," *AB Bookman's Weekly*, 55 (June 16):2866.
"Lilly Library Tributes to Dave Randall," *AB Bookman's Weekly*, 56 (November 10): 2117-2120. Tributes by Herman B Wells and Ronald Randall.
"Obituary Notes, David A. Randall," *Publishers' Weekly*, 208 (July 14): 24-28.
Papantonio, Michael, "David Anton Randall (1905-1975)," *AB Bookman's Weekly*, 56 (August 11-18): 533-534.

1976   "Obituaries. Randall, David Anton," *The ALA Yearbook, A Review of Library Events 1975.* Chicago: American Library Association, pp. 253-254.

PART V

CHECKLIST OF BOOK DEALER CATALOGUES

David Randall was employed in the Rare Book Department of Scribner's Book Store from 1935 until 1956 during which period he oversaw the issuance of many book catalogues. Those catalogues are listed here together with two which he issued under his own name while employed by Max Harzof before joining Scribner's.

Rare Books. The First Catalogue from the Book Shop of David A. Randall; First Editions and Inscribed Copies, Mostly Modern, Together with a Special Group of Volumes from the Libraries of, or Autographed by, the Presidents.

Second Catalog of Rare Books. Book Shop of David Randall. [1934] (Cited in *Publishers' Weekly*, 126 (November 10, 1934): 1770.)

SCRIBNER'S CATALOGUES

Familiar Quotations: A Collection of Their Earliest Appearances. 1935. (Catalogue 102) ("The first catalogue I was responsible for at Scribner's . . . ." *Dukedom Large Enough*, p. 42.)

Catalogue of an Unusual Collection of First Editions. (Catalogue 103)

One Hundred Books. (Catalogue 104)

First Editions of Famous American Songs. (Catalogue 105)

Catalogue of Books Modern, Old and Rare at Reduced Prices. (Catalogue 106)

First Editions of Juvenile Fiction, 1814-1924. 1936. (Catalogue 107)

Scribner Firsts, 1846-1936. (Catalogue 108)

First Editions of American Literature. (Catalogue 109)

First Editions of English and Continental Literature. (Catalogue 110)

50 Books, Manuscripts, Music. [1938] (Catalogue 111)

Bach to Stravinsky: First Editions of Music. (Catalogue 112)

Science and Thought in the 19th Century: A Collection of First Editions. [1938] (Catalogue 113)

First Editions, Rare Books, Autographs. (Catalogue 114)

American Historical Novels, Fifteenth to Nineteenth Centuries: A Collection of First Editions. (Catalogue 115)

Catalogue of an Unusual Collection of Rare Books. (Catalogue 116)

The Modern Library in First Editions. 1938. (Catalogue 117)

One Hundred and Fifty Years of English Literature, 1788-1937, Chronologically Reviewed in First Editions. (Catalogue 118)

First Editions: Johann Sebastian Bach, Ludwig Van Beethoven, Johannes Brahms. (Catalogue 119)

Famous Operas from Lully to Richard Strauss. (Catalogue 120)

First Editions of Music: Important Recent Acquisitions. (Catalogue 121)

American First Editions: Autograph Letters and Manuscripts. (Catalogue 122)

The Limited Editions Club in First Editions. [1939] (Catalogue 123)

Science, Medicine, Economics, etc. In First Editions. [1940] (Catalogue 124)

American First Editions, Autograph Letters and Manuscripts. (Catalogue 125)

English Literature: First Editions, Manuscripts. [1941?] (Catalogue 126)

First Editions of Music. (Catalogue 127)

English Books Printed Prior to 1700. (Catalogue 128)

The Birds of America from Original Drawings by John James Audubon. (Catalogue 129)

Rare Books. (Catalogue 130)

Nineteenth Century Pamphlets; With an Appendix of Wiseiana. 1945. (Catalogue 131)

Literary Manuscripts and Autograph Letters of Eminent Authors. [1946] (Catalogue 132)

Music First Editions. (Catalogue 133)

Checklist of Modern First Editions. (Catalogue 134)

Rare Books in All Fields of Collecting, 1467-1947. (Catalogue 135)

Fifty Distinguished Books and Manuscripts. [1952] (Catalogue 137) ("The last major effort of the Carter-Randall Scribner axis. . . ." *Dukedom Large Enough*, p. 53.)

Autographs. [1937] (unnumbered)

A Catalogue of Original Manuscripts, and First and Other Important Editions of the Tales of Sherlock Holmes, as Written by Sir Arthur Conan Doyle. Together with Important Biographies, Pastiches, Articles, Etc., and a Few Extraordinary Association and Unique Items. [1937] (unnumbered)

First Editions. [1938?] (unnumbered)

First Editions of Juvenile Fiction. [1940?] (unnumbered)

Books on Art, Architecture, Furniture and Decoration, Costume, Textiles, etc., As Well as Sets and General Literature, At Special Prices. (unnumbered)

Americana, Voyages etc. 1939 Selection from Henry Stevens at Scribners.

Americana, Voyages etc. 1940 Selection from Henry Stevens at Scribners.

Scribner's also issued a *Rare Book Bulletin*, a *Rare Book Bulletin*, new series, and a number of *Sales Lists* during Randall's tenure with the firm.

INDEX

207

ABOUT THE AUTHOR

DEAN H. KELLER (B.A., M.L.S., Kent State University) is Associate Dean of Libraries and Professor of Library Administration at Kent State University where he has held several positions, including Head of the Humanities Division and Curator of Special Collections, since his appointment to the staff in 1958. In 1966/67 he held a Lilly Fellowship in Rare Book Librarianship at Indiana University, and in 1989 he was an exchange librarian at Aristotle University in Thessaloniki, Greece. He is a member of several library and bibliographical organizations, and has served as editor of *The Serif* (1964-1975), as book review editor for the *Bulletin of Bibliography* (1982-1990), and on the editorial boards of *Credences* (1980-1984) and the *Steinbeck Quarterly* (1975-   ). Articles and reviews have appeared in a variety of professional journals, and among his books are *An Index to the Colophon* (Scarecrow, 1968), *A Fool's Errand* (Scarecrow, 1969), *An Index to Plays in Periodicals* (Scarecrow, 1971) with a Supplement in 1973, a revised and expanded edition in 1979, and another Supplement in 1990, *Libraries in the '80s* (Haworth, 1985), *Reading and the Art of Librarianship* (Haworth, 1986), and *'Bubb Booklets': Letters of Richard Aldington to Charles Clinch Bubb* (Typographeum, 1988).